The
Meaning of Life….

(It was right under our noses the whole time)

A treasure map to transcend and ascend.

A beginner's guide to enlightenment.
A journey of self discovery to self mastery.

PREFACE

My dearest Seeker,

I have written this book to provide you with a map. A map of remembering, traced by landmarks of struggle, breakthrough, unfolding and awakening.

These pages aren't meant to be followed step by step like instructions, but rather to spark something ancient inside of you. Something that was always there, waiting. This book is your treasure map. Your landmarks and keys will be unique to your path. The dotted lines are here, and the compass is offered, but the treasure is yours to find, and I promise it is closer than you may think.

You may find yourself in these words. You may meet parts of yourself that were buried. Perhaps it will unlock a new level and timeline for you. You may be shocked at what we call enlightenment, for it is not somewhere we go, but what has always been here, within.

Don't rush, take your time. Pause and reflect. Layer by layer, let it unfold. Let your nervous system soften, and your heart open as you walk these paths. A trusted map to remind you of the way home.

Learning your energetic signature

Hey, look at you, beautiful! You're here, showing up for yourself.
That already starts you on the right path! Taking time to connect with yourself is an essential part of the unfolding.

Your energetic signature is a unique vibrational pattern of your soul. Your energetic vibration shows up and speaks before any words can. It is a blend of your emotions, thoughts, intentions, patterns and essence. This can shift depending on your experiences and surroundings.

Be AUTHENTIC. Authenticity is the heart of alignment. Actions, words, and values are all fully aligned with your true self. To live authentically is to choose your full truth over performance. This means to not adapt someone else's energy unless you truly want to. So many of us learn to wear masks to feel safe, to please, protect, fit in, and hide. Each time we step into someone else's version of who we think we should be; we scatter our energy. Authenticity calls your power back. It is the act of saying, " this is who I am, this is what I feel, this is my truth". Self love is an act of courage and strength! When you are aligned with this state, your energetic signal will send that out, and that is what you will receive back. Like attracts like. It's how others can recognize you. Your radio signal that you send out for others to tune into, who are a vibrational match. When you are resonating at the frequency of LOVE, TRUTH, and light- that frequency becomes your shield. YOUR baseline. Lower vibe experiences may try to reach you but they simply cannot sustain themselves in your field, or you simply won't allow it. Allow your HEART to be your filter. Notice how your experiences FEEL. This baseline is your barrier and signal. It will let through what resonates, and what doesn't will dissolve or not become anything in the first place. This book is going to help you notice where you may be shifting out of your baseline energetic signature for someone else, and guide you back to it if you have wandered away. No more playing small. This doesn't mean your ego gets to decide you are better than anyone else. Far from it actually. It simply will keep you in alignment so you experience life perfectly for YOU. The real you is the one holding the controller. Consciousness; the soul beyond the ego's avatar storyline.

Now let's look at the opposition; an example; if you have a fight with your partner before going to work, and if it's unresolved; that upset will carry with you and possibly show up at another time in the day. You may smile less, or perhaps your shoulders are tense or your body positioning seems to drag. Not clearing this energy will dilute our signal, and we won't send the right messages to others. A lot of our day is filled with energetic transactions. That driver that cuts you off, your coworkers, and even your children if you're a parent; these encounters can leave residual energy in our field if we aren't tuned in, and we unknowingly allow the energy into our space.

When we are aligned with our true authentic signature; we can respond to the world from an aligned state. Full of love and compassion, and the willingness to stay true. Not only for others, but for OURSELVES.

THE EGO SELF VS. THE SOUL SELF

The ego is not your enemy. It is your built in survival tool. Think of it as your mask you wear in the world. A costume. One of them anyway! It's the voice in your head that says, " I am this name, I have this job, I own these things, I must be safe."

It is formed to navigate life. This identity gives you a sense of me versus you. It watches for danger and tries to keep you alive. The ego loves rules, comparisons, and " shoulds".

The ego actually limits us. It is rooted in fear, attachment, and separation. It tells you that you are this body only and a personality. It resists change out of fear of the unknown. Beyond the ego, you are pure awareness. The soul, the witness, the eternal spark. The ego is like a small wave on the surface of the ocean. It believes it is separate, but in truth; it belongs to the infinite. Transcending the ego doesn't mean to end the ego entirely. It means to see and notice it, and know when it is in the driver's seat and running the show. Gently remind it that it doesn't need to fight for survival every moment. We can expand beyond it, and choose to live from love, presence, and connection. Not the ego's old stories. When you transcend the ego, you don't erase it; you place it in service of your soul. The ego becomes a loyal servant, instead of the master.

So how do we know if the ego is running the show, or the soul?

Comparison; when we feel jealous when someone else succeeds thinking we are behind or not good enough; *Control;* the needing to be right and to win arguments, or to make others see things your way; *Attachment;* the defining yourself by possessions, job titles, or looks, *Fear of judgement;* holding back your truth in case people won't like you; *Scarcity mindset;* believing there's not enough love, money, or opportunities for all; *Defensiveness;* taking feedback as an attack, or needing to prove your worth; *Conditional love;* loving others only when they meet your expectations. But when we live from the soul; we live from *Celebration* and we are genuinely happy for others' success, knowing abundance is infinite, *Surrender,* the letting go of control, trusting life's timing and flow, *Authenticity,* knowing you are not your labels, but a limitless being, *Courage,* speaking and living your truth even if not everyone understands, *Abundance mindset,* the believing and knowing there is always enough, because you are connected to Source; *Openness,* receiving feedback as growth, not as a threat, *Unconditional Love,* loving everyone without trying to fix, change, or control them, *Alignment,* is acting from your inner guidance, instead of the ego voice of fear. The inner battle is real. The ego is sneaky. It requires consistent presence. To respond to life instead of react. To ponder and reflect instead of making knee jerk choices from fear. We learn to master the pause. In that pause, in that stillness, is where truth resides. EGO says: I need to prove myself. SOUL says: I already am.

EGO: (🔑)
-loud mind chatter
-anxious
-is only about the "self"
-reactive and angers easily
-fear based thinking
-always rushing and hurrying
-lusting and longing
-gossips and talks about others
-can't let go of the past or stories
-takes things personally
-needs to prove itself
-unconscious to patterns, habits, and behaviour (and the effects they'll have on others)

SOUL:(🔑)
-accepting
-loves unconditionally
-trusts intuition

-grateful
-slows down and enjoys each moment
-compassionate to each soul's journey
- know the soul's truth

There are many other traits I could add to these 2 lists, but I am sure you are seeing the difference. Alignment feels like flow and expansion, where ego is misaligned and feels restrictive and controlling. Did you ever ask your friends as a child to make a whirlpool in the swimming pool growing up? When you all travelled around and around and created a large circular flow, and then you tried to go in the opposite direction? Remember that resistance? That's what ego can feel like in life. SO GO WITH THE FLOW!

In this book, we are going to shift from our ego self, the made up false self, and become the soul; the one aligned with our own truths of our heart, and then it will allow us to do the same for others.
I am sure you have heard of the term auric field at one point in life, and if you haven't; I am so glad to be the one to share it with you!
Our auric field is our energetic signature expanded. Some indigenous use what is called a medicine wheel. I will briefly share both!

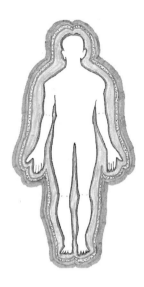

When our energetic signature is shielded and stable; we don't allow misalignment into our field.

Your auric field is a living, multi-layered signal. Each layer performs a distinct function. It has the ability to sense, and memorize, and send out silent messages. When all layers are clear and integrated, you will feel grounded, resilient, and easily aligned with your highest good and highest guidance. If a layer becomes dense or leaky, life shows you where to heal. Through sensations, patterns, and even health signals; our body is communicating.

LAYER 1 is our <u>physical layer.</u> It is just outside the physical body. About 1-2 inches out. It is the energetic template for physical health. It vitalizes the physical with life force energy, or prana/chi. When your body receives steady life force, it will heal better. If this energetic layer is out of balance; you may feel chronic fatigue, have poor sleep patterns, frequent illness, or sensitivity to weather changes. If emotions are left unacknowledged; the body remembers.   Ground more by walking barefoot and practicing mindful exercise.

LAYER 2 is the emotional/feeling layer. It holds both your expressed and suppressed emotions. We wear our heart and emotions on our sleeve. It holds feelings, emotional memory, and relational imprints. It is your emotional weather map. This layer informs how you emotionally respond to life and how you connect with others. When clear, you feel emotionally resilient and compassionate. If it is out of balance you may feel mood swings, or reactivity. This layer is more visible than any of the other layers. Unresolved anger, grief, shame, or sadness will cause a leak in this layer and allow more negative experiences in. FEEL TO HEAL!

LAYER 3 is the mental layer, and it expands out past the emotional layer. It houses beliefs, thought patterns, and mental habits. It is how you interpret the experiences in your life. Clear mental fields allow discernment, where an imbalance could be negative self talk or limiting beliefs, or obsessive thinking, and this will cloud this layer. Our thoughts can become emotions. A blockage or leak in this layer can affect how our energy flows into the inner layers and cause distortion. Make sure you speak for the highest good of yourself and others. Don't let others gaslight your truth, and don't gaslight yourself.

LAYER 4 is the bliss body/astral layer, and it is our bridge from lower energies up to higher spiritual information. This layer can translate subtle impressions, dreams, synchronicities, visitations, and higher guidance. The layers of our auric field are similar to a nesting doll. Multiple, interwoven layers of light that surround your physical body. This layer can store deep attachments, heart connections and soul contracts, and energetic cords both healthy and unhealthy. Wounds here are often related to heartbreak, betrayal, and a disconnection from love.

The next layer is the *etheric template.* It holds the higher blueprint of your physical and etheric body. Your higher self. Your oversoul. Trauma and long term stress, and energetic attacks can show up here and create rips or holes. The next two layers are our high spiritual layers. The celestial layer and the causal layer. We will go over these deeper in BOOK 2! These are where we experience unconditional love, divine inspiration, and connection to Source. You connect to your soul's purpose, karma, and highest timeline. If there is a breach here; you will feel a loss of direction, or feel disconnected from your soul's path. Energy flows from the outward layers inward and then back outward; ideally in balance.

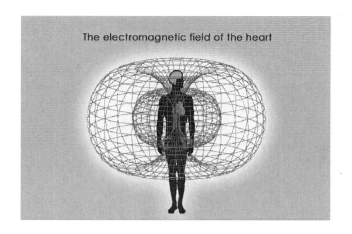

The electromagnetic field of the heart

Do not allow unresolved emotions to remain stuck in the emotional layer; that distortion can affect how thoughts form in our mental layer, and cause discomfort in our physical layer. This can lower your vibration by creating stress chemistry and triggering our nervous system, and then we create a ripple and a loop that won't stop until it's cleared. This cycle can happen over and over and over and create a fog around our field.
We are not going to let that happen! We are going to stop this cycle AND heal the layers where an imbalance may have already occurred. Practices to release emotions like journaling, crying, movement, and breathwork will help immensely to align your connection to self and Source. Visualize a white blanket cloaking you in love and protection. Be kind to yourself while rewiring your limiting beliefs. When we do all these

things regularly, the leaks will repair and you stop physical symptoms from starting. Each day you will get brighter and brighter. We create a new neural pathway for a more positive way of thinking and living.

This takes us to our energetic hygiene!

This is essential for remaining authentic and aligned. We can keep our energetic layers clear and maintained by daily grounding and clearing. Salt baths are an amazing way to be held physically because the body relaxes more, and salt removes toxins out of the body. Our emotions can get swept under the rug and can penetrate the energy layers, causing stored trauma and eventually dis ease.
You can stand or stay seated and do a shake and sweep. Shake your arms, hands, legs, and wiggle that body! You can use your palms to sweep your energy field. Brush your hands over your body and imagine the energetic dust just falling away. Salt, in addition to the bath can also be made into a paste and you can wash your hands with it, or even place some on your third eye area. Do a breath reset! Inhale deep, and exhale twice as long, or even longer. Inhale what we need, and exhale all we are releasing.
Singing, humming, toning, and clapping are quick ways to clear your field AND raise your vibration.
You can even change your clothes, brush your hair, and GO HUG A TREE!

This book will guide you on how to clear things before they even have a chance to manifest. But first we need to diagnose a leaky layer, or a layer with a hole. It is simply a place where subtle energy that should stay contained; leaks or drips out, or sneaks in from an external force. Holes are normal, everyone has them. Some common leak locations are the lower belly/sacral area; we lose our boundary of our self worth and sexual energy. Don't give away your sacred energy to just anyone and everyone. It is meant for connection. Our upper belly is our solar plex (we will cover these more later), and it governs our willpower and sovereignty. The heart area can cause emotional leaks when we pick up others feelings, or if we don't acknowledge our own.

The medicine wheel is another interpretation of how we can balance ourselves and live from alignment. Similar to the auric field; the medicine wheel was created to teach us that we have four aspects to our nature. The physical, mental, emotional, and the spiritual. We need each of these to be balanced for us to be a happy, healthy, aligned human.

We have discussed the ego, we have discussed the soul; let's get reacquainted with ourselves all over again!

Start by tuning into your body; where does energy flow effortlessly and feel like yours; not borrowed? When in alignment, you will feel timeless, deeply present, and in flow.

What are some of your favourite things? Is it connecting with loved ones? Your pet(s)? Perhaps you like art or reading books! Whatever these things are; we are going to start carving out time to do them! This book is here to remind you to start filling your own cup and your own bucket; FIRST. Choosing you.....

Start to deepen your connection by taking YOURSELF on a date! Whether that is spending time with nature or by going for a walk, ride, hike, etc. Heck, go out to dinner and even a movie! You could also reflect with journaling. Write down moments you felt most aligned, or even any misalignment. WHAT LIGHTS YOU UP? DO THAT! Look for repeating themes. Energy shows up in our body as sensations and emotions. When you know yourself and your energetic signature; you can sense foreign energies quickly (what's not you). It allows you to hold your centre during interactions, instead of merging or scattering and saying yes when you actually mean, no.
Scattering is when we leak our energy in many directions to survive, people please or keep the peace.

Merging is when we absorb someone else's energy and emotions as if they are ours. Our nervous system has been trained to seek acceptance and safety in others. Energetically it dilutes our energetic signature and weakens our frequency. We are going to reprogram that!

Now that you've tuned into what is right for you, and what alignment looks and feels like; let's look at what pulls you away!

Contrast and triggers are tools and clues on our map. Without contrast or opposition, there is nothing to learn from for our growth. Everything would always remain the same. Learning from these triggers, and recognizing how they directly affect you, will help you understand the edges (limits) of your own energy signature and allow you to anchor and maintain it. Staying true to your centre and your soul's resonance is a gift once achieved.

The Nervous System and Regulation tools (these are co-ordinates on the map)

Honour the body's signal. A " no " is the body in truth. We are going to express, NOT repress! It's time to tune into your inner map. Our environment can and will shape our frequency if we allow it. You can either be feeding yourself with uplifting and fulfilling experiences, or you may find yourself in an environment that is mirroring a negative response. When we are in alignment and stay true to ourselves; we can control how we show up AND respond in our environments without losing ourselves. I like to look at it like a game of catch. What does the ball represent? Communication is co-creative. The conversation you had wasn't just you speaking to them, but you both tuned into the same wavelength. What does it reflect? What kind of company are you keeping? Do they support your highest path? Maybe you've become rootbound like a plant that has spent too much time in a small pot.

When you stay true to yourself, it is possible you may find yourself not wanting to connect to certain wavelengths anymore because they don't match your new frequency and it's not in alignment to fake it.

Conscious vs. Unconscious Energy Matching:

Unconscious matching happens automatically. You walk into a room and people are laughing, and you smile without even thinking. Or maybe your body tenses up in a room that is sending out negative vibes?

Conscious matching is when you choose to meet your environment in the moment. Meeting other souls where they are, or inviting them to meet you where you are. You consciously soften your body and soften the tension. Let's look even closer at our beautifully designed messaging system....The NERVOUS SYSTEM!!!!

FIGHT mode is reactivity, anger, frustration and irritability. The body gears up to attack. The energy surges; the jaw tightens, and muscles stiffen. Resolving what triggered us in the first place is crucial. Our body will store that trauma and cause dis ease; remember? Do yourself the biggest favour, and heal it and seal it immediately. We can discharge it from the body by taking a walk, going for a run, or shaking and dancing it out. Talk to someone about it, or take some time to do breathing. Focus on the exhale; with each long exhale, the body gets lighter, and you will even feel yourself sink lower into yourself. Even pressing your palms together like in prayer, or placing your hands on your heart will signal safety.

FLIGHT mode shows up as anxiety, restlessness, and the urge to flee a situation. The body prepares to run. You may have a panic attack, your heart may start racing, or your breath may shorten or get faster or shallow.

We can regulate this again by addressing the trigger that it originated from. Or, try box breathing; inhale for 4 seconds, hold for 4 seconds, exhale for 4 seconds, and then hold again for 4 seconds.

One of my favourite methods is the 5-4-3-2-1 Grounding Method. It uses your senses and brings you back into presence. Find 5 things you can SEE, 4 things you can FEEL, 3 things you can HEAR, 2 things you can SMELL, and 1 thing you can TASTE.

This method interrupts the spiralling thoughts and brings you out of the mind and into your heart. If you need a faster method; press both your hands into your thighs and hold.

FAWNing is when we say yes when we actually mean no. When we over extend ourselves to ensure others are happy. Our body tries to avoid the conflict, and we shrink ourselves for the sake of another. Practice micro-boundaries by saying, "let me think about that" before you make a decision that is out of your alignment. Affirm, my needs are important too.

FREEZE is when the system shuts down. You will feel numbness, indecisiveness, disassociation and a blank mind. Your body plays dead. You become still as to what to do next. Try small gentle movements like wiggling your toes. A shift in temperature like a warm cozy blanket, or a fan moving the air. Start to thaw slowly. Focus on one tiny action at a time.

Sometimes *our body knows* what we need before we do.

When we start slowing down enough to pay closer attention; we can begin **self soothing** and catch our emotions and feelings before they go unacknowledged, or projected onto someone else. **Self soothing** movements are innate ways the body regulates itself, and it is often below our conscious awareness. They say so much about how we meet the world and seek safety. Here are some common, and extremely subtle cues that our body talks….

And I must confess; I do some of these too. Now that I have the awareness of these signals; I can provide my body and soul with what it needs to ensure I remain in an aligned state.

-Foot rubbing/wiggling is used for comfort and grounding. I have caught myself doing this most nights at bedtime.

-Hair twirling/stroking helps calm the mind and create a repetitive and soothing sensation.

-Body rocking or swaying can be a gentle motion when anxious or tired.

-Humming and quietly singing or even talking to ourselves will vibrate the vagus nerve and calm the nervous system.

-Rubbing hands together or even holding our own hands creates warmth and physical reassurance.

-Touching our face, cheeks, lips acts as a grounding point, and brings attention inward.

-<u>Blanket snuggling</u> and wrapping up creates a cocoon effect that signals safety to the body.

I invite you to try and notice the small things you do when you are tired, anxious, or seeking comfort. This will allow you to become aware of your natural self-soothing mechanisms; your built-in medicine. A lost art of subtle connecting. We may even reach for something without knowing what and why we are reaching, or maybe we touch our face a lot and fidget. Once we learn them; we can start using them intentionally instead of subconsciously. No one wants to be sending out the wrong messages to people!

The PARASYMPATHETIC nervous system is a branch of the autonomic nervous system. The part that works automatically without us thinking about it. It is responsible for rest and digestion, and helping our body calm down, restore, and conserve energy after stress or activity. It is the brake pedal of the body. To tap into this; we just need to signal safety and calm.

Sometimes others are the cause of our misalignment, and sometimes it is ourselves. But before we go into the Parasympathetic shift; we need to talk about:

TRIGGERS(🗝).
Triggers are tools! They are a clue within your treasure map. The growth activations they create! Work with

them, not against them! There are no bad experiences, just lessons for learning. They help us learn more about ourselves, and what we don't resonate with!

It points back to a wound, an entry point in our auric field! Something unmet or unhealed, or an old protective pattern. If we self regulate without identifying the trigger; we heal at a surface level but the pattern will loop and come back. True healing is when triggers are expressed, not repressed. Bring them into your awareness, and work through them in a healthy way.

I created what is called an emotions jar. I cut out a picture of a butterfly net and glued it on the front. We want to catch these emotions! They are like evidence left at the scene of a crime. The crime being the trigger! I labelled one side Body Mapping; ask yourself how the emotion feels in your body. Where does it sit? Fear-throat, anxiety- stomach. The other side was labelled with a colour chart; what colour does the emotion feel like? Blue- sadness, Red- anger, Yellow- joy, Black-heavy, depressed, Green- content and peaceful. You can also doodle the emotion. I keep some small pieces of paper nearby so myself, or my kiddos can write the emotion down and pop it in the jar! Don't hold them in. I can almost guarantee they will percolate up again or make you sick. Find a way to connect with yourself, so you can face your triggers head on.

Triggers will activate the nervous system. This constant state of stress is not where we are meant to live life from. Notice what state you shift into. Trace it back; "when have I felt this before", " what part of me is being protected right now?" Can you find where it was set off?

Journaling (again), is a classic and very effective way for daily presence with your soul. Have compassion for yourself, and never feel ashamed for feeling. Find a safe space or a safe someone, to help you work through what comes through if it feels too heavy to do alone. You are never alone!

Let's look closer at what emotions actually are. They are energy in motion. A byproduct of something else. They act as messengers of the soul, not enemies to be silenced. They are a living frequency that carry information of our inner world. Each emotion moves differently and vibrates at its own frequency, and speaks its own truth. We need to stop labelling emotions as good or bad, and learn to understand them as a teacher. Every feeling wants to be felt, acknowledged, and honoured. When we resist them, they can, and will become blocked energy. Emotions are not burdens to overcome; they are guides to wholeness.
When we learn to listen to them, they stop controlling us and start conversing with us.
The key is not to transcend the emotion, but to transmute it. Let the energy move through the body consciously until it completes the message. Every feeling, when honoured, becomes wisdom.
Your body is not a coffin for stored traumas. Do not allow the energy to be stored inside.

ANGER:

Anger is what percolates up when we feel disrespected, misunderstood, or even violated. Anger shows us where integrity or self-respect has been crossed. Beneath the anger is often hurt, and beneath that hurt is a longing to be seen clearly. Express your needs with awareness, courage, clarity, and protection of what matters most.

SADNESS:

Sadness is letting go. Releasing what no longer serves. It washes away what the soul has outgrown. It invites stillness and reflection, and reminds us that grief is the price of deep love. Sadness cleanses the heart and opens space for renewal.

FEAR:

The message here is that something feels uncertain or unsafe. Not fully understanding the situation. Fear is the messenger of caution. It asks us to slow down and bring awareness to our present moment. When faced with compassion instead of avoidance; fear transforms into discernment and becomes courage in motion.

GUILT:

The message here is a red flag of misalignment. You acted out of your true values. Healthy guilt is part of your awakening. Love wants to guide us back to integrity. But shame is guilt that has turned inward and become an identity. Shame is not 'your' guilt. Shame is you feeling guilty for something you did not do intentionally. Where guilt is something you did knowingly.

Forgiving ourselves, and learning from the lesson will clear this.

Feeling misaligned and carrying emotions can become heavy baggage. Let's work through them and shift to some more aligned feelings!

JOY!!!

You are in harmony with your truth!
Joy is alignment embodied. It expands your field, magnetizes abundance, and heals through resonance. It doesn't require a reason.

LOVE!!!

Love is the base frequency of the Universe. The current underneath all emotions. Every other emotion is simply love, or the lack of, in distortion. Love all of yourself and others just the way you, and they are.

PEACE:
All is as it should be. It appears when all is settled. When we no longer fight the flow of life. Peace is not the absence of challenge, but the presence of trust.

Harmony isn't achieved through control, but with surrender.

GRATITUDE:

You appreciate everything. You realize that your needs are met and you are naturally abundant. Gratitude transforms perception, and shifts our focus from what is missing, and we notice all the miracles. Each thank you is an energetic multiplier, magnetizing more of the same vibration.

COMPASSION:

Your pain is my pain. But this doesn't mean you become the emotion. You simply hold space for the emotion to move through. Compassion is the container where ourselves and others feel seen with the dissolving of any judgement. Compassion opens the heart's gateway wider than understanding can.

BLISS:

Bliss is a feeling of Enlightenment. You are one with all that is. Bliss is the merging point where emotion becomes pure vibration. The soul remembers itself as light, and all energy becomes love returning to Source.

FULFILLMENT:

Fulfillment isn't found in our materials we have. It is found in what we feel when we are fully present. It's the moment our inner world and outer worlds meet in harmony. It is the exhale after long seeking. It is realizing you were what you were chasing. True fulfillment is sustained by your connection to self, to purpose, and to Source.

Create a worksheet to identify the triggers and emotional events you may have experienced.
How does your nervous system respond; does it remind you of anything, and how can we safely express this instead of repress it? Pause and then reflect..

Love languages and how they're interconnected 🔑

When we know our love languages and live from a state of presence; we are able to tune into the love languages that others speak. It gives others a chance to speak the way that is aligned for them without us expecting them to be a certain way. When we know our love language, and others; we can communicate with each other a lot easier and this can help avoid triggers. Love languages are another example of how our nervous system seeks regulation and security. Receiving love in a way that truly speaks to you will fill your heart and soul, where disconnection can trigger the nervous system. If your relationships can't find alignment in a language you can speak that works for each of you, then the possibility of incompatibility is present. At the core; we all should be loved and feel safe. Love someone for who they are, and not who you think they should be.

The five love languages- words of affirmation, acts of service, receiving gifts, quality time, and physical touch; are more than preferences in a relationship. They are energetic pathways that directly influence the nervous system.
When we receive love in a way that is aligned with us; our body will feel expansion, safety, and stability. When we experience lack, we experience stress responses such as anxiety, withdrawal, or hypervigilance. Once we become aware of our own love language, and that of others; it helps open up the communication lines.

WORDS OF AFFIRMATION are kind, caring, uplifting phrases that we can say to others. There are no judgments. Hearing that we are loved and appreciated can uplift someone that speaks with this language, and when they feel seen and validated; they will want to continue doing things for others without any resentment building. Spread kind words wherever you go, even to strangers. Telling someone you like their hair or outfit can change their day. Many of us are all going through this thing called life, and we have learned coping skills and masks to hide our true feelings and we certainly don't want to put any negativity on someone else's plate.

ACTS OF SERVICE is when someone lightens someone's responsibility load. The body experiences relief. We tend to carry the weight of the world, and offering to help someone could go a long way. Our nervous system learns that we are not alone, which will take us out of survival mode, and allow more time for rest. Offer to help someone that has a long " to do list " by running an errand, or even drop off a prepared meal.

RECEIVING GIFTS is an amazing way to let someone know you are thinking about them. Or maybe you yourself may even enjoy receiving a thoughtful gift. It doesn't need to be a large gift, or expensive gift, to say, hey, I saw this and I thought of you. This tells the receiver that they matter and are valued and cared for; reducing stress and isolation. Surprise a loved one with a heartfelt gift and watch what happens.

QUALITY TIME is when you spend time with your loved ones. Focused presence where you feel seen and heard, and of course; so do all parties involved! This limits the emotion of loneliness, and shifts the body into openness and receptivity. Make time for your family and friends away from distractions by having a game board night, movie night, or even physical exercise with a walk in nature.

PHYSICAL TOUCH stimulates oxytocin (we will touch on this more a little later); the bonding hormone. It can lower the blood pressure, slow the heart rate, and immediately signal safety and belonging. Safe, and approved touch helps discharge stress from the body. Hugs, hand holding, and even a gentle hand touch on the shoulder will send acknowledgement of care to the one receiving it.

Each love language is a nervous system doorway into safety and connection. When these needs are met, the body shifts from survival into expansion. This creates a foundation into exploring subtle energy. Love is not only emotional. It is psychological, spiritual, and energetic. Meeting love prepares your vessel into higher levels of

consciousness.

LIMITING BELIEFS (more co-ordinates)

What is a belief?
A thought repeated over time until it is believed and felt as truth.
Limiting beliefs puts us out of alignment and affects our energetic signature. Whether the belief was put there by someone else, or even yourself; these thoughts need to be healed and released. We are not the voice in our head.
If you are able to catch yourself during a negative belief; ask yourself " Is this true? "
If you are not able to find proof, then it's likely not true!

How do we work with limiting beliefs?
Awareness can help us catch the pattern. Trace the root of it. Where did this come from? Childhood trauma? Society rules, expectations and pressures? Or old wounds from a toxic relationship or a specific experience can show up. Sometimes a thought pattern is a coping mechanism we create to feel safe or accepted and we use it because it feels familiar. We tell ourselves things (sometimes made up things), so specific events make sense and when things make sense, we feel safe. This is how the brain works. When we can become aware of it and heal these patterns; we release the internal programming that binds us. Instead of fighting it, bring yourself compassion. Thank the old belief and tell it you don't need it to protect you anymore. Insert a positive affirmation instead - It only takes one spark to start a fire-

I am worthy of love and success!✔
I have special skills to share! ✔
My energy attracts wonderful people, experiences, situations and opportunities! (as within, so without)✔
My life is full of love, joy and peace, and for that I am grateful!✔

I am the creator of my own reality, and I choose to manifest the best for myself!✔

I am capable of achieving anything I set my mind to! ✔
I choose to anchor and lock in my next level of timeline instead of falling back into potential!✔

Let's come to our senses!

Such a gift to be able to touch, smell, see, hear, and taste!

The gift of SIGHT allows us to detect lights, colours, movements, and see the beauty that is hidden among us. It can also show us perspectives. We can see opportunities, patterns, visions, and truth.
Having the ability to TASTE things is probably a favourite of most! So many yummy options! Our brain is also able to program a memory from taste and smell! Taste provides pleasure and nourishment, and allows us to savour life and receive.
SMELL as does taste, travels straight to the limbic system. The part of the brain that governs memory and emotion. While sight and hearing have to go through the "thinking" part of the brain. When you experience a new smell or taste during a meaningful event, the brain binds them together. Later, when you smell or taste it again, it awakens inside of you as a "felt" experience. Use smell for aromatherapy to create the environment in your work space if you work with clients.
TOUCH helps us register texture, pressure, temperature, and even safety of an environment. Heated blankets soften our being and relax us physically and mentally. Touch can be a way to communicate, take 'feeling' to another level when connecting, and it can even be a way to learn boundaries. Touch is an amazing way to heal yourself and others. Healing

techniques like massage, reiki, therapeutic touch, and pranic healing use our life force energies known as "chi", and "kundalini".

HEARing helps us to listen, but not just to others; to deepen our intuition. It detects energy, vibrations, warnings, and harmony. While it is amazing to hear things from others; aligned actions should always be what we recognize as truth. Hearing signals to your heart - I am connected to my environment.

Let's also not forget about those non-verbal cues. This allows us to tune into our intuition. We are able to pick up if someone is lying, and read someone's energy and intention.

Non-verbal facial expressions are as simple as an expression that reveals true feelings, a split second frown before a fake smile; raised eyebrows that can mean curiosity or skepticism, or furrowed brows that represent concentration or anger.

Eyes can give away a lot. They are the windows to the soul. Eye contact shows interest, challenge, connection, and confidence. While avoiding eye contact can mean shyness, discomfort, contemplation, or guilt. Looking down while speaking can signal embarrassment and avoiding conflict. And of course we all know what the eye roll means!

The positioning of the body speaks too. Keeping a distance, or closeness can signal intimacy or uncertainty, where an expansive posture takes up space. Sometimes we make ourselves small so as to not draw attention to ourselves.

Tune in and notice if you are clenching anywhere; your jaw, your hands, or your shoulders. Holding tension is a signal of imbalance.

Even our vocal cues can say a lot. Volume, pitch, pauses, and tone all say things without saying things. Sometimes we blush, get goosebumps, tremble, and even sweating are ways that our body speaks for us. A beautiful journey of the senses. Every sight is an invitation to witness beauty or contrast. Every sound is a frequency that can calm, excite, or inspire you. Every taste is a way to savour the present moment. Each scent carries a memory and emotion. Every touch reminds you that you are here, embodied and alive! Life is a symphony. An orchestra of sight, touch, sound, taste, feelings, and aromas. Your body is the instrument and your breath is the conductor, and your soul is the one listening. You are literally a walking tuning fork of your own. One that takes in vibrations, and one that gives out vibrations. Your environment matters. Just like tuning forks ring louder when near another fork of the same pitch; being around people, music, or places that enhance YOU will help you be your truest version.. You don't have to do it alone! Let your tuning fork ring true in your tune! This is what it means to live "awake". To turn the ordinary into the sacred. Stop rushing through existence and let life touch you. This is how you become more of yourself!

The Clairs - expanding beyond the senses

Most of us were taught that we only have the five
senses. But our energetic nature gives us an extended
set of senses. Meet the Clairs! French word clair,
meaning clear. These are our intuitive senses that the
soul uses to communicate through our body. When we
activate our Clairs; we can tune into *SUBTLE ENERGIES.*
We are more than our physical form. We are a field of
living light in constant motion. Subtle energies are the
unseen currents that flow through and around us. They
are whispers from the field, and can influence our
thoughts and emotions.
Every feeling, every thought, and every intention, carries
an energetic frequency. These frequencies ripple
outward and can indirectly influence us and others,
shaping our experiences. When we have practiced our
own energetic hygiene; we can remain grounded and
clear so we can perceive reality in truth.

CLAIRVOYANCE (clear seeing) is our inner sight or
visions beyond the physical eyes. During meditation
and even dreams; symbols, colours, projections, and
lights may appear. These can be a way that our angels,
guides, and higher realms can send messages and
downloads to help ensure you stay true to your soul's
path. Some ways you can strengthen your clairvoyance
are to close your eyes, visualize simple shapes until
they become vivid. Keep a dream journal and watch for

recurring visions. Meditate with candles, clouds, or water, and let your images flow without judgement.

CLAIRAUDIENCE (clear hearing) is our guidance for hearing beyond the ear. Having a knowing of the words unspoken. This can come as a voice of intuition, tones, or even downloads that "drop in" similar to a text message. You can strengthen your clairaudience by sitting in silence and meditation and notice subtle tones, ringing, or even words that arise. Try by asking a question inwardly, and listen closely for a whispered response, a song lyric, or even a phrase in your mind.

CLAIRSENTIENCE (clear feeling) is our ability to feel energy in our body. This may show up as tingles, chills, pressure, or emotions that aren't yours. It allows you to feel energy within yourself and others energy.
You can strengthen your clairsentience by scanning your body; where do you feel your emotions or sensations? Notice how your body reacts when meeting people. Do you feel light, or tingly, or even anxious or heavy. These are signals. Place your hands over plants and see if you notice anything.

CLAIRCOGNIZANCE (clear knowing) is an instant knowing without reasoning. Answers and truths or insights will appear out of nowhere with a deep sense of knowing. You can strengthen your claircognizance by journaling your insights before your mind doubts them. Ask a yes or no question and write the first answer that pops in without analysis. Practice your gut knowing.

Why the clairs are important; just as taste and smell create powerful memory portals; the clairs help expand how we perceive reality itself. They remind us that we are more than just our physical bodies. We are energetic beings that are tuned into an infinite field of information. One big sensory experience as I mentioned earlier! Record and trust even the smallest impressions. The more you pay attention to them, the louder they will become. Look at them similarly like a muscle; when we work them, they gain shape and form and strength. These clairs help you become your truest YOU.

Built in pharmaceuticals!

DOPAMINE is the reward molecule. It creates feelings of pleasure, motivation, and reward. Satisfaction! You can tap into this natural drug by achieving small(or large)goals, listening to uplifting music, practicing gratitude, completing daily tasks, and celebrating and being proud of yourself!

SEROTONIN is the mood stabilizer. It brings feelings of well being, calm, and balance. Get high on sunshine, nature walks, meditation, a warm bath with aromatherapy, or feet up with a book.

OXYTOCIN is the LOVE hormone! When you hug, hold hands, make eye contact, cuddle pets, connect in meditation and prayer; this creates a warmth of safety and comfort and connection.

ENDORPHINS are our natural pain killers. It releases pain, reduces stress, and creates a euphoric high. Exercise such as running, dancing, or breathwork, can help you get doses of this!

ENDOCANNABINOIDS are the bliss molecules. It promotes inner balance, and reduces anxiety, making us feel stable. Practice meditation, yoga, chanting and deep breathing, to settle into this feeling.

MELATONIN regulates our circadian rhythm. It supports deep rest and healing. Reduce screens at bedtime, ensure darkness at night, and ensure calming evening routines.

Many of us have become unconsciously and unknowingly addicted to one (dopamine) or more of these internal pharmaceuticals. We will go over this topic a little bit further into this book.

I have created a few work areas in this book for you to use to deepen your connection.

DAILY DOSE CHART WORK AREA

PHYSICAL-

Serotonin (calm and content) - gratitude, sunlight
My daily dose notes:

-

-

-

Dopamine (motivation) - create, music, tasks
Daily dose notes:

-

-

-

Oxytocin (love, connection) - cuddling, pets, service
Daily dose notes:

-

-

-

Endorphins (reduce stress, sense of well being)-
Movement, dancing, singing
Daily dose notes:

-

-

-

Melatonin (sleep, rest, rhythm)- bedtime routine, darkness
Daily dose notes:

-

-

-

Adrenaline (excitement)- courage, adventure
Daily dose notes:

-

-

-

FREQUENCY

Love (breathing, prayer)
Daily dose notes:

-

-

-

Peace (silence, meditation, stillness)
Daily dose notes:

-

-

-

Joy (play, music, content)
Daily dose notes:

-

-

-

Purpose (creative service, help another)
Daily dose notes:
-

-

DAILY REFLECTION:

Today my body needed……..? Was there more of one
thing showing up than another?

I balanced my energy by doing………..?

Tomorrow I will focus on………..?

Feel free to write in this book, or create a journal using a
similar format. I encourage you to do daily check-ins
with yourself as often as possible, and as necessary.
This is how we remain in a constant state of "witness"
flow and alignment. Auto-pilot can be sneaky. It is ok to
SLOW down.

Now having this knowledge of your internal
supplements- let's talk about *MANIFESTATION!*

When we NEED nothing, we receive EVERYTHING. This is the process of gratitude. Needing takes us out of the present moment and tells the universe we are lacking. When in the present moment, we realize that all our needs are truly met. Embody this state every minute and every day. Presence is your foundation. True manifestation doesn't come from clinging to the future, it arises from embodying fullness *right now!* When you are fully present, you are no longer leaking energy into the past or projecting it into the future. Gratitude is not just a feeling. It is an embodied frequency. I am abundant. Instead of yearning and signalling lack, reflect on what already is. This is the law of resonance. MANIFESTATION is magnetism. The body doesn't distinguish between imagined and real. When you visualize your emotion; your nervous system codes it as truth. This coherence creates a strong frequency imprint. The hardest part is SURRENDERING to the timing. The when will it happen attitude. That is the EGO wanting to control the outcome. Let go of the how and when, and let God, Source, Universe, Field; to orchestrate the alignment. Your role is to co-create. Plant the seeds and trust. You don't dig them up every day to check on them. You may do what I do and constantly check using your eyes. LOL.

When we stop chasing and start magnetizing, and start sitting in presence, our energy stops scattering. Release the need to have, and open the space to receive. Each day find AT LEAST one thing you are grateful for. I guarantee it will be easy. The Universe doesn't speak in words, it speaks in frequency. What we seek is already on the way🖤

SYNCHRONICITY is proof of alignment. It is the universe giving you little high fives and thumbs up to keep going and that you are on the right path. Breadcrumbs so to speak. Watch for repeating numbers like 333, 555, 1111, and so on. (I will provide a number chart and more information at the end of the book)
It is those uncanny moments that feel too meaningful to be a coincidence. It could be the song that plays just as you think of someone, or maybe they text right after you think of them. It is our energy in motion. When we are in alignment, the synchronicity multiplies. Gratitude amplifies them. Eventually, your whole life becomes a conversation with the universe.

Why have I shared all of this?
I promise it will all make sense. We will take a journey now with the map, and circle back to a deeper explanation.

And in the beginning, there was love.......

We are going to take a trip back in time. And we won't just scratch the surface either. This map requires going into every layer, looking at every mask, and peeking in every corner. You have the opportunity to remain complacent and ponder the idea of potential, or you can expand and unlock your highest timeline.
It is time to close the gap.

A sweet baby is born. You, me. Pure, innocent; a clear canvas. Brought into this world with a personality, a list of needs specific to you, and gifts that are meant to flourish and share with others. If we are lucky enough; we are born into a family that loves us unconditionally. We are held, we are protected, and we are safe to be ourselves. We grow up allowed to speak, (and be heard) and act and express ourselves how we see fit, (and supported while doing it).
Crazy clothing tastes, loud voice, opinionated, loving, emotional; all parts accepted. No pressure to be like someone else. We weren't kept small if we showed up too big, or too proud. We grow up fearless, confident, stable, and full of love. So much love that we are able to hold space for others in the same way.
But WHAT IF, that isn't how we grew up?
Maybe your parents were always fighting. Maybe you were or are stuck in the middle of this. Or even worse; maybe your parents yelled at you. This is as far back that the smallest traumas can start accumulating. A child needs both parents to show up with presence and an open heart. Imagine the child like a plant for a sec. A plant needs fertile soil to become strong, and

eventually bloom. Regular watering, and lots of sunshine (love). If you neglect this plant, it will not thrive. We are not one size fits all, and we need to meet our children where they are, and not where we think they should be. Our words cast spells and program their young growing minds. If you tell someone bad things for long enough; they will start to believe it.

If you are a parent; please consider that each word you speak, each action you do; whether it is to yourself, your child, or a friend or family; know that it is programming thoughts into the receiver. Your actions and words are the building blocks for a balanced, or unbalanced child. Even our television programs, electronic devices, movies, books. ALL of the world that we take in through our senses begins to program us. Some of it is inspiring and good, and some is bad, and some things can pressure us and we place expectations on ourselves that aren't aligned and we can lose ourselves in the process. We are NOT the voices in our head. That is the ego created for keeping us safe. The voices telling us things are people we have met, societal programming and expectations, and maybe even programming from our own family.

I feel that it is important to include a very subtle form of abuse in this book, and I feel that many of us have experienced and possibly even used it ourselves at times. MANIPULATION. Manipulation is a type of shadow behaviour. These are often survival tools we use and shadow work (which I will touch on more later) is a crucial part of self discovery and self mastery.

EMOTIONAL MANIPULATION is the way we use emotions to control outcomes or get needs met. This can look like guilt trips, playing the victim, over apologizing to diffuse discomfort, and gaslighting. Gaslighting makes someone doubt their perception of a situation.

When we do our "shadow work" for emotional manipulation, we can directly state our needs, and if they aren't respected, it is wise to remove ourselves from the situation. Practice radical responsibility and own what is yours without shame.

Another method of manipulation is control based. These are behaviours designed to keep us in control when we feel unsafe. This can look like giving someone the silent treatment; punishing with withdrawal. Withholding affection or attention to make someone earn it. Or love bombing is overwhelming someone with attention to secure loyalty. Even scorekeeping is manipulation; who owes who what. These can be transmuted with cultivating trust, practice being vulnerable, and establishing clear boundaries.

Mental manipulation is when we shift blame, minimize the other party or parties involved, twisting facts and using selective memory to "win". Instead; try choosing honesty and practice listening. At the end of the day; we all need to be accountable for ourselves. Someone can be the victim in your story, but what role did you play? Maybe you are the bad guy in someone else's story. Knowing what role everyone plays can help dissolve it back to truth. Then once we know this, we can forgive and move forward. So many souls are harbouring resentment of unresolved situations. Our actions, thoughts, words all create **karma,** which I will go into a bit deeper, shortly.

We can even manipulate OURSELVES. This can look like spiritual bypassing; love and light only without looking at the shadow. Self gaslighting is telling yourself you over reacted or that it wasn't so bad, but in fact, you are abandoning yourself and shifting into FAWN ing.

We can create masks and versions of self. Masks are the personalities, roles, and identities we create in a world that misunderstands our light. Masks help us belong, but eventually they suffocate our true essence that they were meant to protect. A form of self discovery and trying on for size. An illusion of identity of the human experience. The search begins to find out who we are.

From the moment we are born, we begin to explore who we are, and part of that exploration is creating " selves", or "masks". This is natural and healthy: a way to experiment, discover, and grow. Each one teaches you something that feels true and what does not.

The masks are created for survival rather than discovery. These versions show up when our nervous system is running, and we are not in alignment. Trauma can, and will trigger masks. These masks serve the purpose of a need to fit in, or to keep the peace, or even protection to hide our true feelings in case we get rejected. Sometimes we try on someone else's version of self for size. These are all tools that are landmarks on our map to self discovery.

These masks can get heavy because they are formed from fear and not curiosity. The key is to not shame the masks, but to recognize them.

The Masks We Wear- Reflection exercise

Mask/Version of Self/ Why I created it?/ Keep?

1.

2.

3.

4.

5.

6.

7.

8.

9.

10.

If you'd like; go ahead and write straight in this book!
When you come back and revisit this page, you can
reflect on your growth. If you would rather journal this
on separate paper, then that is ok too.

Thank the masks for serving their purpose. I release
you now, and align with my heart.
Be kind and gentle with yourself. Self discovery is
witnessing all the layers and loving them. Call in your
true self: Say, " I welcome the version of me that is
aligned with my soul's truth."

As we walk this new timeline; we are going to re parent
our inner child as we go. Doing check-ins often and
asking ourselves if this is what we truly want.
Reparenting the inner child is the practice of becoming
the safe, nurturing presence your younger self always
needed. We all carry parts of us that are still children-
seeking love, protection, and understanding. When
those needs go unmet, we develop coping mechanisms
or masks for our safety. Gently connect with the inner
child parts, and meet those needs in the present time.
Identify the child within; imagine your younger self at an
age where you felt misunderstood, scared, or lonely.
How old do you feel you are? What do you look like?
How are you feeling? Say inwardly; you are safe with
me now. I am here to listen. You are allowed to feel
everything. This builds trust between the adult self, and
the inner child. Listen without judgement. Let the inner

child express what they needed back then, and also what they need right now. This can show up as words, memories, body sensations, or even tears. Reparenting isn't just about comfort; it is also about providing gentle structure. The inner child's needs want to be acknowledged and met. I will be going into this deeper in Book 2, and I also offer soul retrieval services either in person or remotely.

THE MOTHER WOUND:

The mother wound isn't about blaming our mothers, but to recognize the generational pain and conditioning passed down through the feminine line.
It may show up as the need to earn love. Over giving or people- pleasing. Feeling unworthy, or "too much", or "too little."
We may have a difficulty in receiving love or nurturing the self. We suppress our own feminine energy. When we heal the mother- wound; we reclaim our right to be nurtured and express our emotions and have them seen and validated. Mother yourself by providing yourself compassion, patience and UNCONDITIONAL LOVE.

THE FATHER WOUND:

This wound can show up in our lives as abandonment or absence. Both physical and or emotional. It could be criticism of yourself, controlling, or even unrealistic expectations. Struggling with self-confidence and self worth, and even the lack of trust in authority.

Healing the father- wound means we reclaim our sense of strength, safety, and direction. It is about stepping into our own authority.

Witness this rather than the need to fix. Offer soothing words, " I love you, I see you, I will never abandon you." You can place your hand on your heart while you tell yourself this. Speak affirmations into the mirror, take yourself on playdates, and self soothe with a blanket if it feels right!

Coping Mechanisms:

We are such habitual beings. It is so easy to fall into patterns instead of flow. Doing the same thing; day in and day out. Comfortable, complacent; safe.

Just like thumb sucking, or a soother for a baby; some common coping mechanisms we as adults use are as follows: food, alcohol, cigarettes, drugs, sugar, shopping (we have all heard the term, retail therapy, lol), social media, television, over working, and even routine!

Food can become emotional, substances can help numb and or enhance, social media and tv can be used as a distraction, and rigid routine and over working is a way we can control our environment.

These brilliant distractions temporarily displace us. Whether unconsciously, or by conscious choice. Instead of loving and embodying our environment; we lean into these tools. They offer short-term relief, and prevent us from meeting life as it truly is. Another **unconscious** coping mechanism we develop to keep ourselves safe is self sabotaging. Another "shadow" we need to integrate. Self sabotage is when someone unconsciously blocks their own success. We procrastinate, we strive for perfectionism, or we overcommit. Sometimes we start and quit or we even attract chaos. We can unknowingly get addicted to the cortisol that these moments bring. Even self criticism is a form of self sabotage. It erodes confidence and prevents progress. *Why would someone self-sabotage??* Your nervous system loves what is familiar, not necessarily what is good for you. If someone grew up with stress, chaos, and criticism; that becomes their baseline. When peace or success arrives, it can feel foreign, so the body creates stress again. Manufactured drama to recreate the pattern. Picking fights, procrastinating, and returning to what feels normal. This is where the cortisol and dopamine can get addictive. We tell ourselves negative things, and then we start to believe them and they become our identity. Self sabotaging becomes a way to prove those beliefs true. It keeps you consistent with the identity. Maybe we sabotage because we feel we may betray our family.

This could be a time where you question everything. A doctor might mention a chemical imbalance or dysregulation, where low serotonin can make it hard to feel satisfaction or motivation. Leading to repeating self sacrificing cycles. Trauma can keep the fear centre on high alert, so safety feels like an enemy. There's a hidden payoff. Sabotaging reduces the risk of rejection. Staying broke limits expectations. Staying small may prevent judgement or jealousy. It's like the body saying: "I remember when it wasn't safe to shine, so I will protect you by shrinking." "I would rather be in control of the pain than risk the unknown." "Stress feels familiar, let's stay here." The common denominator with self sabotaging behaviour is the underlying need for safety. Even if it isn't the best choice for us.

Sometimes we can become aware of the reaching and seeking and our patterns and we can offer ourselves an alternative option.

Let's shift into conscious choosing! Pause and notice what you're reaching for, and why. Recognize that it once served you, but may no longer be supportive. Instead of reacting, consciously choose whether to continue, or replace the behaviour with something more aligned.

Every coping behaviour delivers a "dose" of something:

Comfort- (oxytocin) when we reach for connection or affection

Pleasure (dopamine) when we chase rewards or stimulation

Relief (sertonin& gaba) when we seek calm, control, or reassurance

Energy (adrenaline&cortisol) when we procrastinate until the last minute, and then create urgency.
TUNE IN and truly ask yourself- "what am I needing right now?"
Some healthy conscious alternatives:
For stress, try breathwork, meditation, and stillness. For loneliness, try calling a friend, or journal, and spend time with nature. When overwhelmed, try breaking tasks into smaller steps. For boredom, try creative outlets such as dance, art, and learning something new.
Choosing EMBODIMENT instead of escape is to say YES to our experience, even when it's uncomfortable. Breathe through the stress, and allow your emotions to move, and stay present in your body. Loving reality doesn't mean we have to love every " circumstance ", but we can love ourselves through the experience, and open doors for how we move forward. Many coping mechanisms are relational; people pleasing, withdrawing, over giving, and conflict avoidance. When we know ourselves; we can be present in our relationships. We have heard the line: Heal your wounds from your relationship you broke in, so you don't bleed onto others. Just because one relationship provided growth in a particular way, doesn't mean that all relationships will be the same. Yes, it can be hard to remain open after pain or heartbreak, but it holds the space for the great things too. Once we know how we self-soothe and protect ourselves; we can start to see these patterns shape who we invite into our lives- and why. We are the ones that show others how we wish to be treated. Don't put up with less than what is for your

utmost best version of self. Staying aligned with our true energetic signature sometimes looks like saying NO, and pausing before choosing. Respond instead of react.

When we release a coping mechanism that no longer serves us; we will experience some withdrawal symptoms because we no longer have that buffer between what we are avoiding. These symptoms can look like heightened emotions, sadness, anxiety, irritability, and even anger unfortunately. Your body doesn't have anything to dampen those feelings and your cravings can create agitation. You may experience fatigue, headaches and even digestion issues. The body stores anxiety in the stomach. Our coping mechanisms often trigger dopamine, serotonin, or cortisol, and when you stop; your body has to rebalance itself. This can leave you feeling temporarily off. Have self compassion and gentle awareness, and move through these like watching a cloud pass by. It will pass. Projection is a common side effect of withdrawal. It is when we take our own uncomfortable feelings, fears, or traits, and unconsciously place them onto someone else. It is a way that the psyche offloads feelings it doesn't know how to hold yet, but this can end up hurting someone else for no reason. Ask yourself, " Is this really about them, or is this something inside of me?" If you are having a really bad day, and I mean ALL day. This increases the possibility that it is in fact not the outer world, but actually our inner world. Perhaps we have reached a state of exhaustion, and our nervous system just can't handle one more thing, or maybe we left later than we should have and we are trying to blame others and the way they drive being the problem when really we could have just left a bit earlier. The tracing it back method will again work in these types of moments so we don't just shift straight into one of the modes of the nervous system. When we stop projecting onto others, we start noticing our own emotions much more vividly because you aren't deflecting them onto others. There may even be a sting when realizing that this may actually be my shit after all. Owning your emotions may bring up fear or rejection, guilt, or even shame. Projection is protecting you.

Sometimes the things we reach for aren't a coping mechanism at all, but a HABIT, and sometimes even an ADDICTION. Addiction isn't always about substances. It can also be about sensations. The body becomes hooked on the highs and lows. The emotional roller coaster that feels like aliveness, but it isn't. Whether it's social media, validation, food, shopping, oxytocin; the pattern is the same. A temporary fix that leaves the soul emptier after.

As I mentioned earlier, we are very habitual and each pattern serves its purpose. These are all points on the same continuum. They all use the brain's reward loop, but the level of choice and awareness, and sacrifice they require changes. Habits are mostly unconscious. They are efficient and predictable and they serve to be supportive. Coping mechanisms are semi-conscious, and they reduce stress and emotional pain. They are supportive only short term and can cause imbalance if overused. Addictions are conscious and compulsive.

They can help us avoid pain and reality, or sometimes we are chasing the reward of the dopamine hit. Addictions can be destructive, and we can lose control. When a habit is providing healthy options for your growth, they are useful tools. When the habit is for escape and completely unconscious, this habit may actually be a coping mechanism in disguise. AUTO PILOT is a sneaky habit in disguise and if left to its own means; it can, and will run the show. An unconscious loop. It is one of the strongest habits we have. A habit of unawareness. It is the mind's way of keeping us efficient, familiar, and safe. We repeat the same thoughts, actions, stories; on repeat. Without even realizing it, the body has memorized the past so deeply and begins living it for us. Auto-pilot helps us survive, but we are STUCK in the loop. We stop choosing our alignment when this happens. Awareness is our off switch. Every time you pause and return to your presence; you reclaim your power. We have the opportunity to reprogram your life from reaction to creation. Consciousness will take you further than you thought possible. The first step to breaking free is to notice when you're operating unconsciously. Ask yourself: "Am I choosing this, or is this choosing me?" "Is this aligned with my highest timeline, or just programming?" Auto-pilot will run any program you've installed- helpful or harmful; empowering or limiting. They will continue to run until you interrupt the program. You can't shift what you don't realize. But once you realize, you will never unsee it.

Coping mechanisms start as adaptive strategies, and they do help regulate your nervous system to survive a difficult moment. But when this becomes the only way the brain knows how to regulate, we are shifting into addiction. It will lead to escalation, needing more of it, compulsive by doing without thinking, and even dependance.

Here's how the addictive loop works; the trigger; pain, stress, unmet need, or an unresolved wound. The coping mechanism provides a quick fix and temporary relief. Our reward is the dopamine hit by the brain reinforcing the behaviour. Our tolerance level can shift and the brain requires more to feel the same effect. We feed it and then the trigger increases and the cycle repeats. Addiction hijacks your reward system. Dopamine surges every time you repeat the behaviour. Cortisol, our stress hormone, can become something our body seeks in drama and chaos or conflict. When we experience pleasure (or pain), the chemical hit is released from the brain, the brain then says, this is good, I like it, do it again. Then it can escalate to something that reminds the brain of the behaviour, we crave it and begin to anticipate the reward, we act on it, sometimes even automatically, and then the chemical is released again and that hit cements the habit and addiction loop, and when it is repeated frequently, the addiction is in control. Even neutral behaviour like checking your phone constantly and sipping coffee, can become hardwired habits. The brain loves predictability and reward.

Having an addictive personality just means your brain and nervous system are wired to seek intensity, stimulation, and reward more strongly than most. This can look like curiosity, being drawn to intensity, or novelty and excitement. We are highly sensitive and our emotions and experiences are felt more deeply. We can make knee jerk decisions and act impulsively. We can even have the ability of getting hyperfixated and getting hooked on things. Boredom can feel like torture. I would like to include a couple images of how we can unconsciously become addicted. So many things we do these days are like an IV drip system. Some are even invisible and subtle! This is where our self discovery and self realization can merge.

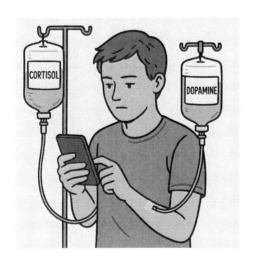

I like to call this the invisible drip. Every day without even realizing it, we are being hooked up to invisible IV bags. These bags drip out the chemicals of our own body: cortisol, dopamine, adrenaline, and serotonin. They respond to our environment, our habits, our relationships, and our screens; both tv and phones. Each device and outlet is feeding one of our natural pharmaceuticals we have access to. It is not always by conscious choice. A notification pings, and the dopamine sends a drip. A fight erupts, and our cortisol surges. A scroll through social media feeds both at once. These chemicals shape our moods, cravings, our addictions, or even the way we perceive love, conflict or safety.

Over time, if we become used to a particular drip; say the constant presence of cortisol from stress or conflict, our nervous system will normalize it. When that stress chemical is absent and disappears, we may feel uneasy, restless, or maybe even lost without it. This is a reason why many people stay in a toxic relationship. The unknown feels foreign. Or we can even seek out a relationship that offers the same since it is all we know. The body searches for what it has grown accustomed to. Over time, the body will begin to quietly ask for it. We unconsciously recreate drama, arguments, or stress because the body is looking for its chemical cocktail. The body is brilliant at adaptation, and will learn to even expect a certain cocktail. Our body can start to build a tolerance and the drip becomes dependance. What used to feel like enough will no longer satisfy. This is why we scroll longer and more often, or we work later, drink more, or seek bigger highs. The drip that once sustained us becomes too faint. This is the seed of addiction. Many addictions can start as the coping mechanisms, but when the body adapts, it will request louder and more, and more often. The drip is neutral. It is our AWARENESS (or lack of it) that determines whether it becomes medicine or poison. Recognizing the slow drip is a key to reclaiming our sovereignty. Awareness lets us locate what we are being fed, and is it mine to choose and keep. Many of us have become addicted to instant gratification. Life is made all too easy. Online shopping with a click; brought to your door. No one barely engages anymore and forces small businesses into closure. Scrolling, sipping, swiping are all validations that momentarily quiet discomfort. While convenience exists at the core; the nervous system learns to crave these microbursts of dopamine. The pinging of the text messages coming in are secretly wiring your brain. Consider keeping your ringer off.

Life is a giant sensory experience. A chemical cocktail. Every glance, every scroll, and every argument is a drip of chemistry into our system. Cortisol, dopamine, adrenaline, and oxytocin, all blending into a cocktail, and we sip it every moment. Awareness gives us back the choice. Am I drinking poison, or medicine?

We are not weak for wanting what is familiar. The nervous system is efficient, and it prefers known states. If your baseline is wired to low-grade stress or drama, peace can feel empty, weird, or even unsafe. That's not failure, it is adaptation. The work is to become your own bartender. Notice the order, change the recipe, and reclaim your palate. The treasure was not in the next hit, but in the stillness you've been avoiding.

Let's do a 5 minute 'drip check" (Practice)

1. Sit or stand comfortably. Close your eyes.
2. Place a hand at your heart and take some breaths in and out. Do this a few times.
3. Ask yourself what drip is running right now? Cortisol? Adrenaline? Comfort? Don't try to fix it. Just notice where your attention lands. Speedy heart, restlessness, tight jaw, cravings to check your phone?
4. Name it, and feel your body respond. Offer yourself a chance to replace it with another option.
5. Do this with patience on a daily basis.

Practical, tiny, and doable steps can be integrated daily. Consistency rewires your baseline. Schedule a daily 2 minute drip check. Replace one reactive habit with a conscious one for one week. Phone ➡ walk, scroll ➡ journalling, or yelling ➡ pause and breathwork. Who pours this cocktail when you feel triggered?

Fasting isn't just about food. We can do mini fasts from things that are pulling on our energy. For those adventurous readers; let's go a little deeper. Here's a practice to try. Think of it as a reset button for your body's chemical cocktail.

DIGITAL FAST (1 hour): Put your phone down. Notice the craving to check. That's dopamine calling. Breathe through it.

CORTISOL FAST (5 minutes): Step away from conflict, noise or busy mode. Sit quietly and feel what it's like to not feed stress.

FOOD FAST (skip one snack): Let your body rest instead of constantly digesting. Drink water or tea instead. Notice how clarity arises.

When you're ready to uplevel this practice; spend half a day without your phone, social media, or tv. This will show you how often your hand reaches out of habit. Each pause will rewire your system. If you thrive on stress or conflict, try 24 hours without fueling it. No arguments, no rushing, no multitasking. Watch what arises in quiet. To uplevel a food fast; skip one meal consciously. See and feel how it is giving your body space and clarity. This is NOT about deprivation. It's about reminding yourself that you aren't controlled by the drip. Fasting isn't a punishment. It is a loving reset. Telling your nervous system it is safe and has all it needs right now.

These aren't bad traits, they just need conscious direction. We are wired for intensity and depth. Our energy is naturally passionate and focused, and sometimes when something hooks us; we go all in.

Let's turn these habits, coping mechanisms, and addictions into conscious super powers.

Let's identify the patterns, understand the gift hidden in them, and offer ourselves steps for growth and purpose. This is who I am, and I am willing to work with it. Let's make a list of the things we consciously want to be addicted to, things that nourish your soul. Instead of scrolling we can channel that energy into writing and creating, or instead of overthinking, pour that passion into a project or service work. Instead of food or sweet treats, try dancing to your favourite playlist or breathwork for regulating. When we reach for something outside ourselves, just simply ask; "Is this something that is truly aligned with who I am, or who I am becoming?" Maybe there is something else we can reach for instead.

Let's ask ourselves this: " Is this a need or is it support?"

It's easy to believe we *need* things to survive. Food, friends, money, or even validation. The truth is; we don't need any of these things to feel whole. We are already complete, and already connected to the Source that breathes life unto us. These things we reach for are actually support. Our food supports the body. Friendships support the heart. Learning supports the mind. They're all treasures along the path, but they're not the destination. When we think we "need" something; we risk becoming attached. Believing that without it we are broken or lost. When we see everything as support, we can enjoy it without clinging. We stay light on our feet to move freely through the map. Attached to nothing, but connected to everything.

Here is a simple DETOX method for doing a reset to feel lighter and brighter:

MORNING RITUAL:
Start each morning with a minimum of a litre of water. Add lemon to it, and even some ginger or turmeric. Turmeric is amazing for inflammation, and when mixed with the others; your skin will GLOW. I have had random strangers stop and tell me how bright my skin was. Ginger is great for aiding digestion. This combination will invite you to visit the bathroom so perhaps keep that in mind while beginning this, or any detox.

Avoid processed food, refined sugars, and alcohol. Fruit is loaded with water and nutrients. Make a smoothie or even grab a fruit tray on the way to work. Try green tea and nuts or seeds for a snack. Green tea is great for helping stimulate your metabolism.

Aim to have veggies at lunch and dinner and a light protein. Lentils, beans, or wild caught fish if you choose.

Here is a small grocery list (try to consciously choose foods from the earth):

- Blueberries (reduces inflammation and makes your skin creamy)
- Cucumber
- Turmeric
- Coconut water (not from concentrate)
- Green tea, herbal teas. Dandelion is great for a liver cleanse and urinary tract infections, peppermint is great for relaxation.
- Quinoa
- Seeds: walnuts, pumpkin seeds, chia seeds, etc.
- veggies like kale and spinach. These are high in iron and other minerals.
- Beets are another great food for reducing inflammation

STAY HYDRATED. I drink a minimum of 1 and a half litres a day, but there is an online chart that helps with an amount aligned to our body type and height and weight. It helps to add a pinch of Himalayan pink salt, or Celtic sea salt to your water. This replenishes trace minerals that get flushed out during a detox, and it also helps our body absorb the water so it gets into our cells. Now that we have cleansed and reset:

Let's talk about ARCHETYPES! These are versions we may embody over our journey. These are slightly different from masks. Masks are a cover up; hiding. Archetypes feel comfortable and we embody them in a positive way, not from a negative perception. Remember again, these are just another label and patterns of energy that help us grow on our journey to self discovery and self mastery. They are not permanent labels, but characters we meet within ourselves. Each one carries a key, a lesson, and an invitation to go deeper within to our soul's truth.

THE SEEKER is always curious and questing. " Who am I?", "Why am I here?" This version teaches us to be willing to leave the familiar behind and search for deeper truths. Find courage to step beyond the comfort zones. Then there's THE CAREGIVER, THE REBEL, THE LOVER, THE HERO, and THE CHILD. Each one plays its own role in self discovery. Each archetype gives us a language for what we feel. Often our emotions and desires feel big but hard to name. They provide a framework or symbol we can hold onto and explore it intentionally. They help us play with an "identity" and experiment safely until we find what is authentic.

RELATIONSHIPS

Relationships are a great way to learn about yourSELF....AND right out of the gate; I need to mention an extremely important relationship challenge.

RELEASE EXPECTATIONS!!!

Expectations can quietly create pain and resentment. A hidden relationship shadow.

Expectations are like invisible strings we tie to others. We may not notice we are even doing it, and when they don't pull the way we hoped; we feel let down, angry, or even unloved.

The truth is, people are not mind readers. If you need something; speak it! If you hope for something; share it! Be transparent in your relationships. Intentions need to be clear. This is that solid foundation. The fertile soil the tree needs to grow from. Communication clears the fog. Expectation without expression only sets us up for disappointment. When we release our expectations, we allow room for feelings of appreciation, instead of waiting for life or others to perform the way we pictured. We can receive what is with open hands and an open heart. This is where gratitude lives.

Releasing expectations in your relationships brings freedom. Love becomes a choice. Pressure dissolves and all that remains is truth, honesty, clarity and connection.

-Instead of EXPECTING, practice EXPRESSING
-Instead of ASSUMING, practice ASKING
-Instead of DEMANDING, practice APPRECIATING

Take a quiet moment with yourself. Meditate and reflect. Place your hand over your heart. Ask yourself if you are expecting someone else to "just know" what you need.

Have you spoken your needs clearly instead of holding them silently? If you are holding them silently, why? What feelings come up if these needs and expectations aren't met?

Reframe it; how can you express it with kindness? How would it feel to release this invisible string, and let others show up freely without the ego's script?

PRACTICE:

Write down one expectation you need about the relationship. When we give it as a clear expression or request; what happens? Are you seen? Held? Validated? If your needs cannot be met; please do NOT think you are asking too much. You deserve love just as much as anyone else.

Our friends and partners are mirrors of how we see ourselves and how they see us. The mirror they offer us is for personal growth of our self discovery. We are the company we keep. Love yourself and others will too! If we don't embark on the self-discovery part of ourselves, and learn our patterns; the nervous system can show up in our relationships. Your attachment is your nervous system's strategy to learn to feel safe while remaining connected. Vulnerability is scary indeed, but learning to love is worth the risk.

There are common styles that show up. Again, these are all ways our body functions to keep ourselves safe! These styles are the anxious attachment style, the fearful avoidant style, the dismissive avoidant, and the secure attachment.
Let's look a little closer at these sneaky symptoms......

SECURE ATTACHMENT is comfortable with intimacy. We can figure this out. Their nervous system can move through stress and can return to safety without extreme up and down energetic mood swings. I am worthy, you are worthy; needs are normal, and we can work through this. When in conflict; the pattern has a name and each owns their part and it becomes a win-win. In this style of relationship, reciprocity is mutual. However; there are some styles that we can reflect on.

The ANXIOUS ATTACHMENT is hyper-attuned to closeness; separation feels like danger or loss. We have racing thoughts and urgency. Common behaviours are frequent check-ins, reading between the lines, or escalation if needs aren't met. The origin of this pattern is inconsistent caregiving, sometimes attuned, and sometimes not. The nervous system turns up the volume to get care. What can trigger this response in yourself or someone you may know is; delayed replies, cancelled plans, or mixed signals. This can lead to excessive texting, testing, threats to leave, or comparison spirals. Ways to work through this is to pause and regulate; speak "When...... happened, my brain said I'm losing you" "What I need is..........., can we do that?"

AVOIDANT attachment values independence. Closeness feels like losing self. Not cold, protective. De-activation when overloaded; preference for tasks over feelings. Where does this stem from; care that met practical needs, but early self-reliance was adaptive. Core beliefs are that your needs burden others; it is safer to need less. Common behaviours are downplaying feelings, changing subject; keeping exit options.
Regulation during conflict is withdrawing to think; appearing indifferent.

FEARFUL AVOIDANT is the need for closeness, but also a high fear of it. The body says go and stop at the same time. This style is often linked to unresolved relational trauma of frightening and unpredictable caregiving.
Love is chaotic and closeness is unsafe, but distance is lonely. This can cause sudden exits after closeness, and self sabotage when things get good. Safety before story. Build reliable routines. I am getting mixed signals in my body, but I want closeness. I need a pause to stay safe and present. I will be back. Many people show different strategies with different partners. These are just explanations. Safety is not negotiable. We need to take ownership of the role we play.

Here are some common patterns:

CORE FEARS:
Connection can wobble but it is repairable
Abandonment or I am too much
Enmeshment or I am not enough for others
Love = danger- mixed signals

REFLEX STRATEGY:
Signal needs, receive needs, repair quickly
Pursue, protest, amplify signals
Downplay needs, allow space

RELATIONSHIP VIBE:
Warm, direct, flexible
Intense, expressive, seeks proof
Independent, steady, until overwhelmed
Magnetic and inconsistent

GROWTH EDGE:
Keep co regulation and repairing
Self soothing
Share inner world and tolerate closeness
Stabilize safety first.

There is a common teaching to not go to bed mad;
however, in reality, not everyone can process conflict
that quickly, and it requires all parties to be on the same
page. Unresolved tension lingers in the body and puts
our nervous system into low level threat. If it goes
unresolved; resentment can build up and it stacks on top
of each other. Some incidents poke at core wounds;

abandonment, betrayal, or rejection and need more time to heal.

When a relationship feels secure enough, repair will happen quickly. If the relationship environment is unsafe, inconsistent or toxic, repair feels dangerous or fake. Healthy relationships are a co-regulating system, the persons feel safe enough to relax. Protect each other's nervous system and watch for clues; raised voices, sarcasm, walking away, or stonewalling can signal the nervous system to activate. Practice co-regulation by lowering your voice, softening your body, and keeping a gentle eye contact. Relationships aren't meant for never triggering each other, quite the opposite actually, relationships are our greatest teachers. We learn things about ourselves that we wouldn't necessarily learn on our own. When we have a trigger, we notice it, trace it back, name it, and repair it! But what if we don't want to repair it? Maybe it isn't safe?

Honour your truth. Not everything should or can be repaired. Especially if you are doing your part and your partner isn't. Some things, especially our heart and safety, are non-negotiable. Emotional abuse, physical abuse, betrayal, and just disrespect that is ongoing or not addressed are all signals for closure. If you express your needs in a clear and secure way but it is just disregarded, then you have the choice to choose YOU because you deserve happiness and alignment. Sometimes we are just an energetic mismatch. We realize that we are no longer aligned with this particular person's values, behaviours, or their growth path.

Repairing this would just re attach us to an expired karmic contract. There are two sides to this coin. Healthy consequences of choosing to not repair the relationship can preserve your peace, protect your energy, and create space to allow relationships that are reciprocated. Unhealthy consequences if the repair is not dealt with properly; there is a good chance that the same pattern will show up again and again, and then also in any future relationships. The key is intention. Am I choosing to not repair because I am done, or because I am scared?

CO-DEPENDENCY is a relational dynamic where one person's sense of identity, self worth, and emotional balance becomes overly tied to another person. A blurring of where one person ends and the other begins. It can feel like you're living your life through another's moods, choices or approval. It is an attempt to gain love, safety or belonging by controlling the other person's emotions. It comes down to survival. A subconscious strategy learned early in life to prevent abandonment, conflict or chaos. If you are wondering what co-dependency looks like; it is saying yes when you mean no, or worrying too much about what the other is feeling and sacrificing yourself. Co-dependency struggles with boundaries at the risk of being rejected. Having a low sense of self can cause you to feel empty and wonder who you are without the relationship. Don't tolerate toxic behaviours to avoid being left alone. If you grew up in a home where love felt conditional, your system will have learned how to FAWN. You avoid rocking the boat, and seeking validation. This keeps the body in a subtle state of vigilance, scanning for cues about how the other person feels so you can stay safe. From a spiritual perspective; this kind of relationship creates an energetic cord of attachment. The loop begins; one is the giver and one is the taker until awareness is brought and the cycle is broken. Healing this cycle will help you return to sovereignty and interact from wholeness rather than need. As I mentioned earlier; the familiar, even if toxic; feels safer than the unknown. Maybe we are attached to the identity we have and are in that particular relationship and we are scared to lose our "self".

Our attachment style is our relational fingerprint of the nervous system. The way we learned to stay connected and safe with others. It requires you to understand your wiring, so you can choose new and conscious ways of relating to others.

Our attachment style is not a fixed destiny. It is a living map of the ways we learned to seek safety and connection. The power lies in recognizing our patterns, regulating our nervous system, and choosing new responses that align with the love we truly want to experience. When we raise our frequency, our field begins resonating with new realities, new choices, new possibilities, and possibly new people. If the other person's vibration stays the same, it can feel like you're no longer in the same room. Communication might feel strained, and shared dreams no longer align, and even intimacy can feel energetically off. This isn't punishment; it's resonance. Two frequencies either harmonize or they don't, and ascension naturally reveals where harmony exists and where it does not. It can feel like you are losing them, but in truth, you're simply feeling the contrast between you. Sometimes you can love someone from a higher state while staying physically close. It just can't, and shouldn't compromise your energy.

Just like our food choices affect the health of your body, relationship choices affect the health of your field. Your heart, mind, and energetic state. Imagine that plant that has become root bound in the pot. It needs to be upgraded to a bigger pot with new soil and more nutrients. When it's root bound it can't absorb the water or nutrients. A toxic friend or relationship can have the same effect. Are you thriving and blooming? And remember; rejection is redirection. When one door shuts, another will open. Spend time with people who match the vibration you wish to hold. Notice if you feel drained, and lovingly set boundaries. Keep your soul's signature clear and aligned with your true self so you don't get pulled into other's frequencies. Trust your own energy, and your truth.

PERMISSION SLIP:

You are allowed to choose yourself.
You are allowed to walk away.
You are allowed to not repair.

You do not owe anyone endless access to you.
You are free to close the chapter when the lesson is complete.

Conscious partnership can become one of profound
growth, healing, and awakening.

I am going to offer you a new perspective on how you
look at your relationships. It will help you bring full
presence into your relationships. Our relationships are
a mirror. A mirror that will reflect to us what we are
accepting, or not accepting and what we are learning
about our partners, and we are also learning about
ourselves!
When you know yourself so deeply, as I mentioned
earlier; we show each other how we want to be treated.
This includes, and is not limited to; what we tolerate and
what we don't. These mirrors can reflect to us where we
may be complacent for the sake of comfort, or reflect the
most amazing love to us. The mirror effect is when the
people, experiences, and opportunities start showing us
things. What we believe about ourselves, what we are
ready to heal, and what we are broadcasting through
our frequency. When we pay attention to the company
we keep; we get a snapshot of our current vibration.
This isn't about judging ourselves or others. It is about
noticing patterns. What does this situation say about
where I am energetically? What in me might be calling
this in? This is where your sovereignty comes in. You

always have the power to shift, to re-align, and to choose who and what you interface with.

We hold the keys to choose our path. Most relationships are karmic relationships, or a soul mate relationship. A twin soul relationship can be up for discussion, and left to the ones in the relationship. Twin soul relationships have been misconstrued, and they actually represent the highest level of love with God. These styles of relationships all serve a purpose for our highest good. Even the ones that don't feel good!

Karmic relationships are for clearing karma. They are often a bumpy ride, full of lessons and conflict, and not to be mistaken for punishment or reward; they are for us to awaken to the loops and patterns. They will have emotional highs and lows, and an imbalance of energetic exchange and when they fulfill their purpose; we break the cycle and move out of them, completing that level of growth for our soul's evolution. Some karmic contracts are short-term, some last a lifetime, and some dissolve once the lesson (or lessons) is learned. Once we awaken to these patterns and loops; we can be aware of them much sooner and accelerate our soul's growth and healing.

A SOUL MATE is someone whose soul resonates with yours in harmony. They are meant to support your growth, mirror your gifts, and help you expand into love. There are many types of soul mates in our lives and they can be romantic, platonic, family, teacher, or even a brief encounter. It is a soul to soul and heart to heart connection. This type of relationship can endure the test of time because of the peaceful state of it. It is when the soul seeks to evolve that turbulence can show up. This can be a common thing in relationships; especially ones that we enter at a young age. It is normal to outgrow a relationship. We can thank them and send them love, and continue to honour the relationship at a distance, but it isn't always in our highest alignment to stay.

Briefly exploring TWIN FLAMES; two sides of the same coin. Two sparks that split and took separate journeys of growth. While this relationship is the highest form of love stories that ever existed; the true purpose of this relationship is about accelerated evolution. Become your highest alignment. Twin soul encounters stir up deep emotions, joy, pain, and longing. They reflect parts that are needing to be integrated so you can become your true wholeness! When you create your inner union of your masculine and feminine polarities; you may experience this in physical form as well.
Not everyone has a twin soul, and that is ok! No one is missing out when in alignment. It comes down to what your soul agrees to before incarnating. What lessons and paths were for your highest evolution.
Your soul will grow perfectly with its own chosen path. If you find yourself obsessing; bring your focus back to your own healing.

THE NARCISSIST AND EMPATH

Narcissistic relationships are one of the most potent spiritual initiations we can experience. They reflect our own need to remember our own worth, our boundaries, and our voice. This very common dynamic begins with intensity, magnetic chemistry and it can feel like destiny. They are often drawn together because the empath is the giver and the narcissist is the taker. The taker that is seeking validation, admiration, and control. The taker reflects the light of the empath but not for the empath's sake, but for the taker's sake. This bond forms trauma resonance. The empath's inner child wants to be chosen so it gives. This actually drains the empath's life force energy through manipulation, control, lies, co-dependency, and self-betrayal.

There is an extreme push and pull that happens here. Go, wait, come back, I am sorry. Over and over and over. The empath being so trusting and forgiving; easily falls into this loop. Leaving this style of relationship is crucial. Forgiveness doesn't mean letting them back into your field. It means releasing the energetic contract that kept you bound. The love you gave so freely was never wasted; it was a reflection of your essence.

MASCULINE AND FEMININE - THE INNER DANCE
(a landmark for the treasure)

From wounded to DIVINE ARCHETYPES
THE *DIVINE MASCULINE* & THE *DIVINE FEMININE*

If we recognize the mother wound and or father wound within ourselves; it gives us the opportunity to move through them. Our awareness is the first healing. The true invitation is to grow beyond them. We awaken higher expressions of the feminine and masculine within us.

Our divine feminine energy emerges when we heal the wounds. Instead of people- pleasing, or self-abandoning; we choose to embody compassion, intuition, creativity, and unconditional love. We allow ourselves to receive, to feel, and to trust the natural flow of life.

Our divine masculine energy emerges when we heal the father wound.
We stop controlling, demanding, seeking approval, and instead, we; embody stability, protection, presence, and direction. We create safety- not by dominating, but by holding steady, and showing up with integrity.

Together, these archetypes create balance. We are nurtured and supported(feminine), and we receive guidance and support and empowerment from the (masculine).

This inner union is what allows us to grow strong and whole. Never depleted. The tree that has strong roots, and sunlight.

The next time you see an old wound surfacing; pause and ask:

" What would the Divine Mother say within me right now?"
" What would the Divine Father say within me right now?"

Over time we learn to parent ourselves with unconditional love and unwavering support.

THE TREE OF YOU.........

Notice yourself as a tree. The roots in the ground. Is it fertile? Do the roots go deep to solidify the trunk? Notice your trunk, notice your branches. Is there strength? Where are you seeing your strength? Perhaps you have strong roots, a sturdy trunk, or branches reaching high.

Is there any crookedness? Maybe there wasn't enough light, and your branches had to grow and reach out in a weird way to get light shining on them. Or maybe the branch bent to someone else's light. Maybe you were cut back too harshly. Kept too small. Kept small to fit in a space you were too big for? Ask yourself; what kind of care, sunlight, or nourishment do I need now? A haircut or maybe some trimmings? It is time for you to grow straighter, brighter, stronger, and more vibrant. The work isn't to cut down the tree, but to notice where it has bent, and to offer support, and to guide it toward the light again. Healing is less about fixing what's broken, and more about nurturing what's already there.

When we master our inner masculine and feminine energies, and create an inner union within ourselves; we become a conduit for that same balance in an outer reunion in the relationships that we cultivate.
Sometimes we may lean towards, and embrace one energy more than the other, and they both serve their purpose. We want to embrace BOTH as wholeness, not as a specific ROLE that we play.

MASCULINE ENERGY has qualities of structure, logic, protection, focus, clarity, doing/action, and providing and giving. If a feminine is functioning in her masculine; she inadvertently will force the man into his feminine. A masculine energy needs purpose and drive to fully step into himself. The feminine should let the man lead when possible, and when he is allowed to lead, he's choosing fully from his heart, but of course it's ok to dance. The masculine loves purpose and the feminine guides him to his heart and to serve with purpose. This action guides her to soften and give her love freely and unconditionally.
When masculine energy is imbalanced; there will be rigidity, domination, aggression, and avoidance of emotions.

FEMININE ENERGY qualities are nurturing, intuitive, receptivity, and flow. She loves to vibe, and be in the

ultimate essence of all of herself. She trusts the masculine to provide and care, and she surrenders to the flow of life and trusts the unfolding that the divine has planned.
When feminine energy is imbalanced; she will be manipulative, chaotic, and over sensitive.

In a healthy rhythm, we ebb and flow between both energies depending on the environment. Our inner masculine can set boundaries for ourselves, and your inner feminine can nurture us after. Healing isn't choosing one or the other; it is learning to balance and harmonize them inside ourselves.

The union of our inner masculine and feminine energies is one of the first steps towards wholeness. This union within gives us the ability to fully love and provide for ourselves from a full cup. We then can give to others from that full cup. We learn that we have all we need within, and that we don't need to seek it from others. The key has always been in our hands. From there we can move into the greater rivers of energy- chi, kundalini, and the chakras without being pulled out of balance. This inner union has also been called yin/yang, shiva/shakti, and of course; Adam and Eve. On the surface, they're portrayed as the first humans, but in deeper traditions, and my personal perspective; they represent the polarities within creation.
Adam, the divine masculine principle. Consciousness, logic, structure, awareness, and the seed.

Eve, the divine feminine. Intuition, emotion, creation, receptivity, and the womb.

Together they form the union, and during their separation; the soul descends into duality. Forgetting oneness. When they eat the fruit, they're awakening to self consciousness; polarity, choice, consequence, karma. It's not about sin, but the soul learning discernment. When these two find their way into union; we harmonize and return to Eden, the inner paradise, unity consciousness; bringing heaven to earth-Enlightenment.

OR.....PLOT TWIST.......Maybe they were twin flames? Maybe each of us has a divine counterpart planned for by God. We all have perspectives and the wondering is magical. We don't need all the answers. Just have fun with the perspectives!

When it comes to relationships; here are some questions you can ask yourself:

" What in me feels awakened by this person or connection?"

" What does this relationship teach me about myself, my needs, boundaries, or desires?"

" How can I integrate this energy within myself, whether or not they are physically with me?"

Try some heart activation exercises and tools that can help you be open and not closed off in a relationship.

HEART ACTIVATION TOOL BOX:

Random acts of kindness! Without needing approval or applause!

The heart is a sensing organ first, and a feeling center second. Practice feeling before figuring. Consistency matters more than intensity. Small daily heart led offerings build a safe and steady frequency. Especially for the extra cautious hearts. You can have an open heart while shielding with boundaries. Heart activation without boundaries can leave you depleted. Especially if it's not an equally reciprocated relationship. In this case, you can tell your partner that you love them but you need some space to care for yourself. Place your hands on your chest in the heart area, and ask yourself what your heart is needing.

Cacao is a heart opening medicine. A chocolate flavoured bean grown in tropical regions on a tree. It is considered a superfood due to the large amount of nutrients it contains.

Yoga and somatic movements can also open the heart. The posture known as bridge, even supported bridge, opens our heart. Gentle backbends, and opening arms to the side, and even with bent arms.

Laughing opens the heart AND raises your vibration. Crystals like rose quartz, and plants like roses and jasmine, and others are supportive.

You can do partner and relationship applications. Use ceremony or daily heart practices with your partner to co regulate. Sit face to face, breathe together, then share appreciation. You can reflect and discuss what values you honour in each other, and if there's room for improvement, that is ok too. This is how we grow. Don't let your ego take it personally. Acknowledge your partner's needs may not be exactly the same as yours, and as their partner; you love them the way they are unconditionally.

REFLECTIONS............

What does my heart ask for in quiet?
Where am I giving my heart away? Is the energy exchange equal?

How do I feel when I receive love? Is it unfamiliar? Too much? Too little?

Sometimes when our heart activates, it may stir up grief or old emotions. Allow the tears, and rest for recovery. Your heart is generous, not a dumping ground.

CHECKPOINT

Let's do some integration journal pages…….

- List some coping mechanisms I have transformed
- What patterns have I recognized?
- What relationships or lessons feel complete?
- What qualities am I calling forward as I step into my next chapter?

Feel free to go ahead and write in the book. You can always use a pencil if at another time you would like to review your responses.

-

-

-

-

-

-

-

-

We need to touch on PERSPECTIVES:

The many lenses of life. Our personal point of view.
Life, including us, is not one-size-fits-all. We can all
climb the same mountain to the summit, and take our
own aligned path there. We each carry a unique lens
through which we experience the world. These
perspectives are shaped by our history, our nervous
system, our beliefs, and our surroundings. No two are
exactly alike.

Perspectives matter because they are how we create meaning. The same event can be seen as a tragedy, a lesson, or even a blessing depending on how our lens perceives it. When we honour each other's perspectives; we can recognize that each person's truth is valid for them, even if it doesn't match our own. This allows judgement to shift to compassion. Perspectives can evolve with our growth. What at one point felt like an obstacle, once we move through it; may later reveal itself by becoming a stepping stone. When we loosen the grip on there's only 1 way, and allow multiple perspectives; we open ourselves to wisdom and growth.

RECLAIMING YOUR SOVEREIGNTY AND LIBERATING YOUR SOUL!!!

SHADOW WORK and INNER WORK are an essential part of self mastery. We have to fully clean the house. We can't fully step into mastery if parts are still hidden. We have to look at the repressed parts to heal them, reflect on them, forgive them, and integrate them so they can be released. True alchemy. To start reclaiming and taking your power back; we need to do the inner work, including the shadow work. Shadow work is the process of uncovering, facing, and integrating the unconscious parts of ourselves. The thoughts, patterns, masks, archetypes, and beliefs we have just discussed must go under the microscope to be seen, integrated, and released to allow wholeness.

Things we have rejected, hidden, or suppressed. The shadow holds both pain and potential; the very keys to your wholeness.

Notice when you are triggered, emotionally charged, or feeling resistance. Remember; alignment feels like flow. Pause and witness the reaction rather than immediately suppressing it or projecting it. Ask, "Where have I felt this before?" "What is my body telling me?" Have compassionate curiosity. Why did this part of me show up? Validate the inner child's needs and feelings. We have to trace it back. Find the origin, and find the entry point of the wound. Kind of like a sliver. Is this childhood memories, cultural conditioning, or even past experiences? We need to give the shadow the validation. We need to give love, safety, and expression to the trigger. Reframe the old beliefs. "I am not enough" becomes "I am worthy as I am" Turn pain into power.

Ask yourself what you may be avoiding, or where do you feel shame, and what part of me needs MY LOVE right now. Imagine sitting with that version of yourself and listening to what it would tell you. Look into your own eyes and speak forgiveness, truth and affirmations. Shadows are not evil. They're disowned energies; old wounds, and fear based patterns and trauma fragments, but also a gift. A glimpse into healing and setting your soul free. Ask your shadows with love; "What do you want me to know?" "Are you protecting me?" "Are you ready to be set free?" The lost becomes found, and the wounded is healed. In essence, a shadow forms any time an aspect of yourself is rejected, feared, shamed, or not allowed to be fully expressed. Either caused by you or the world around you. The most common cause of shadow formation is childhood conditioning. You were taught certain feelings were bad, or too much. You were only praised for being good, quiet, or agreeable, so other traits get buried. Trauma, neglect or emotional absence creates inner fragmentation. Our sensitive self becomes a shadow and will surface later in the form of an overreaction or shutdown. When a moment is too intense to process, a part of our psyche splits to survive. This can be caused by abuse, betrayal, violence and neglect. These parts go underground until it's safe enough for them to return. Each shadow holds a piece of your original essence. A lost voice, a sacred truth, or a deeper love. When you heal a shadow; you remember who you were before the world told you who to be. What parts of yourself do you judge or try to hide from others? Are there any triggers that keep coming back?

You've explored who you are, how you feel, and how you express yourself. You've remembered your archetype, and listened to your inner guidance. Now it is time to stand fully in your light. You hold the keys to unlocking the kingdom. Sovereignty means you are the ruler of your inner world. No one else's opinions, energy, or expectations get to sit on your throne unless you consciously invite them. Radical acceptance, radical self-responsibility, and radical self-freedom! Stop giving away your power and sacred life force energy.

THE PARASYMPATHETIC SYSTEM

When we live in constant fight or flight, we burn out. The pendulum should swing both ways. Stop surviving and start thriving! Tapping into the parasympathetic is when we switch into rest and digest mode. This is where we heal, integrate, and thrive! This is where we send the signal to our body that it's safe. When the nervous system is calm; heart rate slows, blood pressure lowers, and our muscle tension decreases. The body sends resources toward cellular repair, immune function, and tissue regeneration. Cortisol drops and our own pharmaceuticals can be released. Drink tons of water always as it cleanses the body of toxins, including cortisol. Once digestion and absorption are complete, the body shifts into elimination. This is why it's important to have a conscious eating pattern. Listen to your body. The large intestine absorbs water and prepares the waste for elimination. The liver processes toxins and metabolic byproducts sending them to the intestines and kidneys. The kidneys and bladder filter blood and remove waste through urine. Our body is taking in and integrating nourishment. Physically, mentally, and emotionally. The slate is clear so the next cycle can begin fresh. We are in this state in the morning so it isn't always best to break the "fast". Putting more into your body before it has finished its cycle will cause a backup. When we don't enter this rest and digest state enough, we compromise the system and can get bloated, constipated, a hormonal imbalance, and even energetic and emotional stagnation.

You can't shift what you don't notice. Let's start this new version of you with gentle self observation. Is your jaw tight? How about those shoulders, are you wearing them as earrings? Are you racing through tasks or moving with intention? When you're in this state, your vagus nerve is running the show. Our restoration mode. Let's dive into energetic hygiene. We discussed what our baseline energetic signature was at the start of the book, and now we need to create a practice to keep us at that baseline, and open to higher levels as well! Now I will share a simple map of your sacred temple. Our magical systems that help our physical body function smoothly and in alignment.

Your body is not just a shell you walk around in; it is your living *temple*. Each system is like a room in your kingdom, and together they create a map that leads you back to your soul's true home. You hold the keys to your own alignment, healing, and ascension.

THE CIRCULATORY SYSTEM- *The river of life*
Its physical role is to pump blood, carry oxygen, and nutrients through the body. On a spiritual parallel; it represents flow, abundance and our life force prana and chi energy. When the river flows freely, life will feel spacious and abundant, and if blocked we can feel stagnant and stuck.

Move your body with exercise. Dance, walk, run, sway; just move!

THE NERVOUS SYSTEM- *The control tower*
Its physical role is to send and receive signals. It decides the fight, flight, etc, and rest and digest. On a spiritual level, it helps connect you with your higher self and intuition. It will help you anchor into presence once you begin to tune in. Learning to calm and reset your nervous system is a key to peace, clarity, and accessing higher states of consciousness.

THE RESPIRATORY SYSTEM- *The breath bridge*
Its physical role is to bring in oxygen, and release carbon dioxide. In spiritual terms; the breath is the bridge between the body and spirit. Conscious breathing is conscious living. Breathing is one of the fastest ways to shift your state, open your heart, and feel connected.

THE DIGESTIVE SYSTEM- *The alchemist*
The physical role is to break down our food. It absorbs and nourishes what we need, and discards the rest. If we take in more than our body needs, and if we don't allow enough time for the rest and digest phase; the body will store it until it catches up. Healthy digestion isn't just about food. It can teach us to slow down and savour, and release what no longer serves. When we choose conscious eating in a spiritual way; we can thank our food, and give thanks to the earth for helping it

grow. If another living being gave its life for you; it is absolutely a new level to give thanks.

THE LYMPHATIC & IMMUNE SYSTEM- *The gatekeepers*
These systems help clear waste, fight off invaders, and maintain cellular boundaries. Your body says this is me, and this is not me, and will protect myself at will. Eat healthy foods that are full of colour like a rainbow. Eat living food from the earth. These types of food are loaded with vitamins to keep these systems working at full capacity.

THE ENDOCRINE SYSTEM- *The timekeeper and translator*
This is our system that controls our hormones, which regulate our mood, sleep, cycles, growth and metabolism.

THE ELIMINATION SYSTEM- *The sacred release*
What goes in, must come out. This system helps remove extra waste and toxins through the colon, bladder, skin, and lungs. Elimination is essential for renewal both physically, emotionally, and spiritually.

THE MUSCULOSKELETAL SYSTEM- *The temple walls*
Our bones and muscles are our structure, a foundation that holds us up and allows us to move around.

THE NERVOUS & ENERGETIC OVERLAY- *The circuitry*
This is the brain, nerves, and subtle energy lines. The meridians and nadis. This is your wiring for your

consciousness, where downloads and intuitive hits arrive.

TIMELINES......What is a timeline?
A timeline is an invitation to a potential path your soul can walk. Think of timelines as streams of possibility flowing from this moment forward. Possible outcomes that we can experience. Some are similar to where you are now, and some are radically different leading to a whole new way of being. Timelines are like rivers. Each one flows to a destination that matches its frequency. Some are slow, some are fast, and some are turbulent. When we heal, grow, or make new choices, we can navigate into a parallel stream that feels more aligned. None of them are set in stone, and you shift between them through your choices, thoughts, emotions, and energy.
Multiple timelines exist at once. Imagine standing at the center of a forest with dozens of paths leading out. Each path is a different timeline. Where you put your attention and energy determines which path you step onto. The more you stay focused with aligned thoughts and aligned actions, the more solid it becomes- until it's the reality you are living. Alignment feels like flow. When we make a decision to step into a new timeline; look at it like a GPS map. If you accidentally take a wrong turn, the map will automatically reroute you on the new path to the same destination. Look at it like those choose your own adventure books; when you

make a choice, a sequence of events will happen. If you make another choice, a different sequence of events will unfold. If you are currently on a timeline that isn't serving your highest good, then I invite you to take micro steps to change it. Sometimes we can get stuck in a timeline; complacency. Sometimes our consciousness fragments during trauma, and a piece remains frozen in that moment or that version of self. Our emotional, energetic, or even physical responses are still running on that timeline. We don't grow past that age or experience. An unresolved karmic imprint that keeps looping and replaying so it can be witnessed, loved and integrated. A piece of you is living a different version of your story in an alternate timeline where you feel longing, regret, or even deja vu.

Some emotional signs that you may be living in an outdated timeline are how you respond to your current timeline triggers. Emotions will reveal the age of self that is running the show. Big emotions that feel disproportionate to the situation. Tantrum energy, pouting, or even shutting down. The emotions could even cause emotional freezing, going numb, or even disassociating when confronted with stress. Sometimes the same emotional story plays over and over without resolution and they can't progress past that point. We can avoid change or new opportunities, or anything that challenges their comfort zone. Daydreaming or idolizing the past is a good indicator we are reluctant to be in the present. Let's quantum leap forward!!!

Let's unlock your highest timeline that you are ready for! You can shift to a different timeline at any moment. A single choice, insight, or healing an old wound can start the new path on a new timeline. Your energy is the steering wheel. Your emotional state, beliefs, and frequency are what aligns you with the timeline you experience.

AFFIRMATIONS TO SAY EVERY DAY:

- I am worthy of love and respect
- I forgive myself and let go of guilt
- I am constantly learning and growing
- I am in control of my thoughts and feelings
- I am grateful for all I have
- I am at peace with all that I am
- I am enough just the way I am
- I choose peace over stress
- I trust myself and the path that I am on

HIGHEST TIMELINE:

Write down what your highest timeline looks like. What are you wearing? Is your vibe natural, or do you use makeup or art to accentuate your inner state? Are you fully embodying your choices? Do they feel like hell ya? These vibes need to show up in relationships, career, health, and your spiritual life. You will need to embody it. Practice daily alignment using affirmations, self care, and speaking truth. Take one bold step each day towards that vision today! Trust the process and watch for your synchronicity! Coincidences are alignment in morse code! Love notes from the Universe! When you are walking your highest timeline; you are living in full authenticity, life feels like expansion, not compression. Yes means yes, and no means no. It will provide you with the deepest joy.

Visualize a door that is marked " highest timeline". Your future self is on the other side. You hand yourself a clue about who you are becoming. Remember what it looks like. That is the next step. Those are your next instructions.

When we make gigantic changes, and giant leaps, we call this a quantum leap. It is essentially a progression beyond linear progression. You shift vibrationally, energetically, or consciously into a completely new state of being, or a new timeline, or reality. Instead of climbing one step at a time; you find yourself on a whole new staircase. You make an instantaneous shift, not bound by gradual time. One realization, one choice, or one alignment can propel you into a new version of yourself. Instead of moving along your current trajectory, you skip tracks into another timeline that resonates with your new vibration. You don't identify with the old you; instead you anchor a new reality of the future you. It isn't forced. It is embodied.

How does it happen? Radical decision! A clear and committed choice that leaves no room for the old version. It often comes from a massive insight, or breakthrough. Maybe a spiritual download, or a moment where you just can't stay the same anymore. You don't just shift timelines, you shift who you are. Fear, guilt, shame, or unresolved trauma can anchor you into repeating timelines. Process the unprocessed emotions, release the limiting beliefs. Let go of attachments that hold you down. Trust the process. Let go of how and when and what it looks like, and let The Creator reorganize your reality. How do I know if I have quantum leaped? Things that used to look impossible, feel natural. Habits and patterns that once defined you feel like they belong to someone else. Doors open, new opportunities arrive, and divine guidance feels louder. Your nervous system will eventually calibrate to your new frequency. A quantum leap is choosing and embodying a frequency so fully that your reality has no choice but to reorganize around it.

Shifting into our highest timeline is as easy as raising our vibration. What does RAISING OUR VIBRATION mean?
Let's dive in!
It is a tiny choice that you continuously show up for regularly throughout your day. These practices can shift your field, mood, and clarity.
Dancing, laughing, acts of kindness, bathing, self-care, and connecting with nature are all simple ways to raise your vibration. Eating foods that are the colour of the rainbow, and hydration are very high vibration.

Now let's talk about *KARMA*. What it is, how it works, and how we can work with it. I know I have mentioned the word a few times, but now we will look at it closer.

Once we have an understanding of it, we can move from karma into *DHARMA*.

Karma is not punishment or a reward. It is simply the energy of cause and effect. Every thought, word, and action has an energetic signature, and that energy will ripple out into the world, eventually finding its way back to you so you can learn from it. Think of it as an echo or a feedback loop. It is life's way of holding up a mirror so you can see yourself clearly and grow. Your actions and choices will create the life experiences you have. You can create a positive ripple or a negative ripple. Each path will create the byproduct of your decisions. Every action has a reaction. Karma can feel heavy. Some say karma is tied to the concept of rebirth and may result with conditions showing up in another lifetime. Karma is also to help our soul evolve and level up. Unhealed karma shows up in loops. Repeating relationships, habits, or lessons until we finally recognize the pattern and learn the lesson. Karma teaches us through repetition, where dharma teaches through alignment. Karma keeps us in our nervous system instead of living in intention and purpose. The energy of Karma is neverending. How can we shift into the soul's purpose and dharma? We alchemize the patterns into wisdom. We become the witness of ourselves. We create from conscious choices. We are able to see the outcome of our actions. Dharma is the right path for your soul. The aligned way of living that honours your true nature and your purpose. It is your highest calling, the state in where your actions flow naturally with the universal current creating no new karmic entanglements. When you love in dharma, you will feel deep peace and alignment. Carried and supported by life. Your actions are in service to something larger. Truth, love, and the collective good. It is God's will to serve.

When we become the witness while in dharma, we shift from being a character in the story to the one observing the character. It is a zoomed out perceptive. The watcher.
Instead of identifying with each thought, emotion, sensation, or archetype; we just become aware and watch them like clouds moving by. This doesn't mean you detach from life and disassociate. You simply stop taking every reaction as truth. You become the one who sees rather than the one who is tossed around by the storm.
When you are in karma, you are caught in cycles of cause and effect and reacting unconsciously.

KARMA says: " They hurt me. I must protect myself and lash out"
The WITNESS says: I feel hurt. I see my defense mechanisms rising. I breathe. What actions are aligned with my highest path?"
DHARMA responds with compassion or even walks away with clarity and closes the cycle.

Some practices for entering the witness state are to pause and name any thoughts or emotions. Say to yourself, " I am noticing anger, or I am noticing an old limiting belief."

Anchor into your body, and breathe in and out. Do not react. ZOOM OUT. Visualize yourself watching the situation as if from above. A drone camera, and perspective from your higher self.
What would the version of you that lives in peace do in this situation? Karma lives in the past and future; what happened and what might happen. The witness brings you back to the NOW where *choice* exists. This keeps your energy and your power with you and not stuck in drama loops. You break ancestral and personal patterns. You strengthen your intuition because your inner channel is clear.

Now let's dive into how we can ensure the channel stays clear!
Life is that giant sensory experience we touched on; full of sights, sounds, feelings, and patterns that guide us home to ourselves. There is no one size fits all path to wholeness. We all receive and perceive differently and that is the magic.
Some traditions speak of the chakras, which are energy centers along the spine. Others use the medicine wheel; a circle that honours the four directions of self, and the cycles of life. Modern language calls it the auric field or the nervous system. Each way is the same way to the truth. You are whole, layered and luminous.
I will start with the chakras for your understanding where your energy flows freely and where it may be needing attention.

ROOT CHAKRA ● is the focus of safety, stability, and grounding. The ***key*** is trust, comfort, and presence.

SACRAL CHAKRA ● is the focus of creativity, intimacy, and flow. The ***key*** is flow, feelings, and creation.

SOLAR PLEX CHAKRA ● is the focus of power, will, and confidence. The ***key*** is courage, self love, and boundaries.

HEART CHAKRA ♥is the focus of love, compassion, connection, and truth. The ***key*** is love. Unconditional love without self sacrifice, and the innerstanding of how others may feel if you were in their position.

THROAT CHAKRA ● is the focus of your truth. Express yourself and speak clearly and kindly. This ***key*** is your truth.

THIRD EYE CHAKRA ● is the focus of intuition and perception. Listening to your inner voice. The ***key*** is clarity.

CROWN CHAKRA ✸ is the focus on our connection with Source and Oneness. The ***key*** is full surrender and trust.

CHAKRAS EXPANDED............■

ROOT CHAKRA - Keywords: Grounding, survival, and belonging.
I HAVE

Our foundation. The baseline of the root chakra is our safety and security. Whether we are living from a fear based lifestyle or a trusting lifestyle. This energetic center connects us to the earth, safety, physical body, and survival. It is our survival security. Money, patience, stability. When this chakra is blocked; we will have money issues, addictions, low self-esteem, fatigue, and a general feeling of disconnection from the world. We can do self-care balancing by going for a massage, planting a garden, grounding by placing our bare feet on the ground. Eat root vegetables like carrots, beets, and sweet potatoes. Feeling safe in our body. Trusting that all will be ok. Practice gratitude for what you have. Repeat affirmations like, "I am safe, and I belong".

SACRAL CHAKRA - Keywords: Creativity, pleasure, and expression
I FEEL

This chakra is our energy centre that is tied to our creativity, our feelings, and how we show up in the world. When this chakra is blocked we could be over emotional or emotionally cold, struggle to adapt to change or a lack of spontaneity, sex addiction or no libido at all, rigid beliefs, or holding back in life. Guilt and shame are common for this energy centre. We can realign this chakra by connecting with our body. Dance or sway your hips to music, take baths, and journal your feelings. Allow yourself to feel good!

SOLAR PLEXUS- Keywords are power and confidence
I DO

This energy centre is our confidence centre. Your willpower to persevere in trying times, your self-esteem and self love, and your purpose. This is your light that you share with the world! When this chakra is misaligned, you will have low self-esteem, low energy, stomach issues, and anger. Practices to re-align this chakra can be martial arts, core strengthening exercises, or core breathwork such as the breath of fire. Say affirmations such as, "I am strong. I can."

HEART CHAKRA - Love and affection
I LOVE

This energy centre is associated with the heart! The bridge to the soul. This chakra represents our capacity to give love and compassion, not only to others, but also to ourselves. We have the ability to forgive, be understanding, and treat all as we would ourselves. When this chakra is not aligned we will experience symptoms such as jealousy, bitterness, loneliness, a lack of empathy and compassion. Again, not just for others, but our own self too. We can balance this chakra by practicing forgiveness, dating ourselves, or doing something kind for a neighbour or the community. Activate your heart chakra by releasing emotional blockages. Open yourself to self love and universal love. Balance the masculine and feminine energies within.

THROAT CHAKRA- Communication and truth
I SPEAK TRUTHS

This energy centre is an extremely important one. When we don't speak our truths, or speak in truth; this energetic misalignment can fester within and may make an appearance at a later time in life. If you have difficulty expressing your thoughts and feelings, or a fear of social anxiety; you may have a blocked throat chakra. Physical symptoms can be a thyroid problem, sore throats, laryngitis, or coughing. To gently re-align this chakra, you can try talking to a friend that you dearly trust, or maybe singing in the shower, and even humming can help this chakra.

THIRD EYE CHAKRA- Intuition and vision
I SEE

That gut feeling and inner knowing about someone or something is your key to this chakra. It will take some discernment to know the difference of a trauma response to protect ourselves that the ego creates versus our true intuition. This chakra and the heart chakra work as a team. Trust how things *feel*. When this chakra is blocked you will have trouble concentrating and poor memory. Physical symptoms can be headaches and migraines. Being in the logical, ego mind can inhibit our intuition. To bring balance back to this energy centre you can practice daydreaming, fantasizing about what you would like to manifest. Focus on the present moment. Sit in mediation and connect with your breath. You can keep a dream journal by your bedside. Essential oils like frankincense and sandalwood will clear this chakra. You can place dabs on your skin. You can also burn incense.

CROWN CHAKRA- Spirit and Oneness
I UNDERSTAND - I AM

This chakra is your connection to your higher self, your guides, and source energy. You are divinely guided and never alone. When we have nervous system issues, cognitive troubles, and a lack of purpose or direction; this energy centre will be blocked. Depression and a lack of spirituality hold you back from the bigger picture. Sit in silence, meditation, and prayer on a daily basis. Find how many things you are grateful for. Visualize white light or golden light above your head. Affirm: "I am one with all that is."

ZEAL CHAKRA- THE MOUTH OF GOD

This special chakra, also known as the well of dreams; rests at the base of the skull near the occipital ridge. It is a gateway to higher consciousness and spiritual perception. It is the seat of mystical insight, clairvoyant vision, and our connection to realms beyond the veil. While the third eye is our projector and lens; the zeal chakra is the transmitter and amplifier. It channels the life force (kundalini) energy from the spine and bridges it with higher light frequencies.

It helps us align with divine messages, visions, and dreams. It can help deepen meditation and altered states of consciousness. This chakra helps you align to your soul's mission.

If this chakra has imbalances, you will have headaches, neck tension, or stiffness at the base of the skull.

Practice humming, chanting, toning. Gentle neck stretches and rolling the head can free blocked energy.

The ZEAL CHAKRA is the doorway between body and spirit, earth and sky.

It represents the moment when the soul remembers that life is not random, but a carefully designed commitment that has already been written. It is considered the portal through which divine energy enters the body, bringing higher frequencies into form.

Sometimes called the ascension chakra because it supports enlightenment and multidimensional connection.

While the Zeal chakra serves as a doorway into higher perception; the heart chakra remains the true bridge between the physical and spiritual realms. It sits in the centre of the chakra system. When the heart is open and balanced, energy flows up and down the spine. We have access to higher realms while staying grounded in our truth. If the heart chakra is blocked, we get stuck in the lower chakras and repeat survival based patterns, or even power struggles. Open your heart and allow love to flow both inward and outward, unconditionally. My heart is open and flowing, bringing heaven to earth.

By exploring the chakras, you have traced the map of your inner world. From the grounded roots that keep you safe, to the crown that connects you to the infinite. When these chakras are all in alignment, and your inner masculine and feminine energies are united; your channel becomes clear; you begin the Enlightenment process, what Christianity describes as 'going to heaven.' Christ Consciousness/ One Consciousness. You can begin ' becoming the witness', and co-create your life with God.

This will also cause the **Kundalini to awaken,** also known as your "Life force energy"; it begins to move through your body. If your chakras aren't fully clear, it will feel destructive. Look at it from a housekeeping perspective. If you have kept your rooms of the house untidy, kundalini is the housekeeper that comes and puts everything back into order. Clean and tidy. This means all stored trauma, all ego selves, all unhealthy habits, all unaligned choices must go. Look at it like a giant closing out sale. Everything and anything that isn't aligned with your highest self and the universal law, has to be cleared. It can feel like a forest fire. Burning away the old growth and beginning again new. This entire process is to create space for your truth and light.

Some say the kundalini is like a coiled snake at the base of our spine. It is an energy all of its own and once it reaches the top floor of the house; the crown chakra opens up to our vast consciousness that is available to us. More than you can even imagine. I personally feel that Jesus's halo represented the expanded consciousness. " I and my Father are One, the kingdom is within."

The serpent is kundalini. The Tree of Knowledge represents the nervous system, or the spinal column. When the serpent climbs the tree; the energy rises up the spinal column, into the crown, awakening higher consciousness. Your union with God/Source/Universe, etc! So many labels and perspectives leading to the same result. Trust what resonates with your soul, and leave the rest.

Kundalini symptoms can vary, and while some may be uncomfortable; it is entirely safe and for your highest aligned path. Let the Divine send Its light into you, that you may remember you are one with it.

SYMPTOMS:

-heat
-itchy
-electricity
-involuntary vocal sounds
-involuntary body movements (shaking, shifting, fidgeting, etc)
-feeling the energy in your spine

-emotional releases (anger, sadness, confusion, etc)
-visions
-flashbacks (some from past lives)
-tingling

Each soul and each vessel will experience this process uniquely.

Since it flows along the spine, movements like yoga and dancing and swaying can help keep you comfortable on the days it flows more. It will eventually settle and you can exist normally. Your baseline frequency becomes a lot stronger. You can step into expanded versions of yourself.

It is very important to trust the process and not try to control it. Trust and rest as needed. I can not tell you how long it will take for you. Be patient, eat live foods, and stay relaxed. It may even feel lonely if you don't have someone to talk to about it. You may even feel like you're imagining it; I promise you that you are not. It will rush through you like a rushing river through a canal and cleanse your body and spirit. Your consciousness can expand quite rapidly, and if your nervous system isn't prepped; it will do what is required to balance that. It will need to be integrated with grounding techniques, humility, and care. Once that balance is achieved, kundalini is awakened and aligned within you; it leads us to wisdom, compassion, creativity, and the ability to live in direct connection with Source.

Let's differentiate KUNDALINI from *CHI*, as they are both unique and not the same.

CHI is the universal life force energy that flows through everything. Breath, food, air, and us. You may feel it as warmth in the palms, or tingling when deep breathing, or the vibrations in your body after a hike in nature. Chi sustains and circulates. It is the fuel that supports health and balance. Practices like Tai Chi, Qi Gong, Reiki, yoga, breathwork, and even mindful exercise can build and circulate Chi. It is always moving like wind and rivers.

Chi is like water; nourishing, flowing, and essential for life. Kundalini is like fire. Transformative, powerful, and capable of complete transmutation when awakened. One circulates to keep us alive and one encourages expansion with Source.

My personal testimony journal entry from 2021:

My Kundalini awoke after I made the conscious choice to leave my marriage. A 23 year long relationship with another that had long expired. We had grown far apart and the distance had become too far for us to find our way back. And really, we should never travel backwards. We had children together so leaving a toxic environment wasn't easy. Not only was I experiencing the many layers of grief; I was also dealing with the Kundalini. As any message in life; take what resonates, and leave the rest. To those who don't understand, you may judge, or try to deny, call me crazy, and that's ok. The logical ego mind likes to have things make sense, and when it doesn't, it feels unsafe. You are allowed your perception and so am I. When we haven't experienced something, we tend to fear it, or label it. Whatever we need, so it does make sense. Sometimes we even make things up! This is a safety tactic our body is programmed to use.

Our body has a direct phone line to The All. Our mighty Creator. When we become activated, we open up our super powers such as ESP, and all the Clairs. The senses beyond our normal 5. We begin our ascension process. Many that have walked the earth have become enlightened, and so can we. We have energy centres known as chakras, that if cleansed, will allow our life force energy to travel to our brain. It can be uncomfortable when not prepared. I experienced massive emotional purges and had days I just wanted my life to be over. I know now this was part of the purging and ego death. I had involuntary vocal sounds. My diet changed rapidly. A lot of foods I was eating all of sudden became gross and I would get really sick if I ate it. Alcohol became intolerable, and me being a stubborn soul, tried to push this one, but I promise you; the body will win. I even had tons of involuntary body movements. This of course always happened at night time. I understand now that this was because I was in the rested parasympathetic state so it could do what it needed to do, where in the busy nervous system it slows the process down. My body would flail about like a fish out of water. I even woke up one night with my head at the end of the bed and my feet at the top. You can't stop this process. Don't try. Many nights were spent awake. I had to kneel in the bed and arch my spine like a cat with my head and chin tucked in and just stay there until the Kundalini said it was time to lay back down. One evening I even *felt the energy shoot up my spine like the sledgehammer game at the fair when it shoots up and rings the bell. Now years later it is stable. Sometimes it wants to play and I will dance or do yoga, or even just meditate in presence.*

So why awaken the Kundalini? Unlock the best life you came here to live!

How?.......

It is crucial that you do the inner work. Clear all your chakras. Don't try to spiritually bypass the shadow work. You can do special breathing techniques like the Trinity breath, to move the energy up the spine and expand your consciousness whenever you wish. Connect to God, your oversoul/higher self, ascended masters, and even other realms and dimensions.

We did not come here to play small. You can graduate to many levels of awareness.

Now go love each other, and create something!

In order to ASCEND, we need to UNPACK! LIGHTEN THE LOAD! TAKE SOME THINGS OFF OF OUR PLATES! Starting with MORE SHADOW WORK. The dark and dense icky must go, and I am here to support you through this. We need to create space for the Light. Our bodies are the Kingdom of Heaven. We don't go to heaven, we embody heaven. We bring heaven to earth, through our essence, our presence; our CONSCIOUSNESS. The denser our bodies are, the more weighed down we can feel. If we are too dense there is no room for all the light of heaven. Not just physically, but energetically. This can hinder our ascension. When we shed excess weight, whether it's physical pounds, stored emotions, or energetic baggage, we create space! Think of it like cleaning out a crowded room. Once the clutter is cleared, the sunlight streams in more easily. The same happens within us. Releasing what no longer serves our highest timeline makes room for higher frequencies and continuous expanded awareness. It's not about chasing thinness or meeting society's standards. It is about alignment. A body that feels lighter, freer, and less burdened becomes a more receptive temple for Spirit. We can ascend into dimensions of truth, love, and divine connection. The lighter you exist, the higher you can go. At those higher peaks, the air is clearer, the vision is sharper, and Spirit's voice is easier to hear.

So it's not about perfection. It's about travel. Each release, each lighter step, brings you closer to the treasure.

Let's talk about EGO DEATH.

Ego death is the loosening and partial dissolution of the smaller self. The stories, identities, and defense patterns that have been running your life, so you can unlock your truest self. Unpacking and clearing requires the ego's tight grip to let go a little. When the ego relaxes, energy that was held in fear, shame and protection, can be freed to fuel creativity, compassion and align you with your soul's mission.

You will feel less driven by fear, status and rigidity. Old roles no longer fit. The victim, rescuer, perfect child, etc. There's a sensation of space, some breathing room. Your inner state will feel quieter, have clarity, and even relief. We don't even realize where we are holding onto things. Relationships will shift. Some will deepen, and some will end. Often these people were a version of you that has changed.

First we must surrender. A conscious choice of letting go of control, identity, stories, or habits. We have to have true confrontation with ourselves. Where we maybe have jealousy, rage, grief, or shame. This is the medicine. Triggers are tools, and they are landmarks on the treasure map. An invitation to the party of your soul. When you notice yourself speaking, reacting, or acting; PAUSE, and ask, "Why?" "What is my intention right now?" Are you seeking love, validation, control, safety, connection? Is this action aligned with who you want to be, or an old survival pattern? This question brings your unconscious motives into the light so you can choose from a place of sovereignty.

Start with some shadow journalling. When do I feel the most shame or guilt? Why? When was the last time I allowed myself to be vulnerable, and what was the outcome? What emotions or experiences do I avoid sharing with others, and why?

Reflect on a relationship that caused pain. What lessons can be learned from that experience? How do past traumas still affect my present relationships and choices?

Is there someone I need to forgive? Is it me? Did I have childhood needs that were unmet, and how can I fulfil them now? Am I judging others? Why am I judging them? Am I judging myself? What are the things I don't like about myself? What things DO I like about myself? How can I show myself and others compassion and understanding?

Write the parts of you that you hide, and thank them for protecting you. Write something you are ready to let go of. Maybe you need to release the villain in one of your stories? When we hold someone as a villain in our story, we remain energetically attached to them. Every time we replay the scene, rehearse the argument, or tell the story of how they hurt us and the role they played; we are leaking our power (energy). The truth is; this is a teacher in disguise. Their role, however painful, helped awaken something inside of us. It may have shown us how to make boundaries, or remember strength we forgot we had. Perhaps you gave them so many chances when they told you they would try harder, and this showed you how willing you were to trust and that you have a big heart. Forgiveness doesn't mean agreeing with what happened. It means freeing yourself from the energetic weight of carrying it. The moment you stop needing someone to be the villain, you stop needing to be the victim. You will know when the release is complete when their name or face no longer trigger an emotion, only understanding.

Take your time and do this work at your own pace to ensure it is fully integrated and fully accepted. Do things for others without needing any validation, or praise, or identity around achievement. This work requires regular alone time to dissolve social masks, and meet your true pulse. Explore a passion or interest you neglected. What steps can you take to rekindle that excitement? It only takes one spark to start a fire. We don't need to earn value through our successes. Make sure your intention is from the soul, and not ego. You are choosing to do this for YOU, and not to impress others.

Create your own integration treasure map. Learn awareness. Notice the triggers and stories and write them down. Create a new story, and a new response. This journey requires constant and daily check-ins. Ego death is iterative, not a one and done process. There are layers and layers like an onion, and once you think you know it all, think again. Don't dismiss emotions. Feel them. List some identities you cling to. Labels such as, the good daughter, the survivor, the warrior, the hustler, the mother, and many others. Literally everything is just a label. The ego will get louder in silence once you remove all the noise and distractions. If you're ambitious; try a silent retreat. Away from the noise, cell phones, tv, etc. Instead of running from what arises; witness it. See it for what it is and have compassion. We are going to let the shadows free, this is what they want, and create our new truth.
If intense trauma emerges; please seek immediate guidance. You don't have to do this alone. Find a trusting friend, family member, a therapist, or trauma informed practitioner.

When we have spent a long time in survival mode, we carry heavy bags. I've always liked relating negative experiences like picking things up and carrying them in our backpack of life. This backpack gets stuffed with old beliefs, traumas, fears, and outdated stories. Unpacking the bag and items that are no longer aligned, creates space for clarity, lightness, and expansion.

First recognize the bag, then see how heavy it is. Notice where you may feel stuck or anxious. Is it in your body? Tension, jaw clenching, weight of the world in your shoulders? Maybe you're storing in your heart? Grief, criticism, or resentment? What beliefs are we carrying in the bag? Maybe you feel you're not worthy or good enough. Another perspective is perhaps you haven't found your soul family.

Narratives we repeat- "I always mess things up, and people leave me" Again, not a fault, it's simply a lack of resonance between souls. When you write these down in your journal, it's like taking each item out of your bag. You can sort through things, and decide what stays, and what goes. There is an invisible weight of holding everyone's emotions, even our own. Trauma can even be positive things. Constant busy life routines, and parties, and even vacations can cause trauma. It isn't what we always think. It comes down to the impact it has on our nervous system and how we process it. When we are healing any trauma, we need to locate the entry points. Where did it start? In our minds? In our emotions? These will all be stored in the body. The body remembers. We follow our map to find it and mend it. Imagine how good it feels when we pull the sliver out. Releasing a trauma that no longer serves us has the same uplifting feeling. People, places, and moments can leave a residue. Ask yourself if you have anything residual that is ready to be cleared. What residue are you leaving to others?

It is ok to want to disappear. Take a break. Lots of them. Go ghost mode. Just come back. We will miss you.

Always keep the lessons, wisdom and strengths you gained. Release the pain, shame, and fear that no longer serves you. Transmute trauma pain and reframe them into fuel for the future. This process catalyzes growth.

Every time you unpack, you raise your vibration, strengthen your nervous system, and your ability to stay calm. One step at a time into sovereignty and wholeness.

So what does stored trauma look like?

When we experience an intense experience; it can overwhelm our nervous system, and that energy of that particular event can become stuck. In our tissues, fascia, and even our cells. Instead of moving through us, by addressing it at the time, or after the initial incident; it lingers- a paused vibration. This stored energy can affect us. Our hormones, digestion, and overall vitality.

Common physical signs of stored trauma can be misalignment in your muscles. Chronic tight shoulders, neck and jaw. Persistent low back or hip pain. Our skin and hair can change. We may experience rashes, eczema, hair loss, or thinning, or maybe sudden acne and hives. We may have unexplained weight gain or weight loss. Food cravings or emotional eating. These are ways we are seeking support. We may experience insomnia and frequent nightmares. Fatigue even after rest is a big sign of unresolved energy. Startled responses or hypervigilance is indeed a trauma response.

We may experience irregular cycles, or early perimenopause, or delayed puberty, and libido swings.

Some common immune, or autoimmune responses can look like frequent colds and infections, or chronic inflammation. We can have emotional symptoms as simple as feeling stuck, overwhelmed, anxious, or even numb.

We can help regulate our nervous system with deep rest, and grounding. Cold plunges are great for relieving inflammation.

Somatic exercises like tapping, shaking, and massage help work with the deeper areas of the body.

Clearing and diagnosing trauma is like a process of elimination when discovering a food allergy. You won't necessarily know what a triggering action is at first. Notice the patterns. It will be a process of elimination. Take something away and see what happens, and slowly integrate it back in if nothing shifts. Healing requires honesty and curiosity. This is about listening without judgement, and allowing what was hidden to come to the light. To be seen, loved, and released.

Your body is not betraying you, it is communicating with you.

In events of more intense trauma or more significant events in life; our consciousness can fragment. A piece of ourselves remains frozen in that moment or that version of self. Our emotional, energetic and physical responses are still running on an old program. It's like we never grew past that age or experience. We may have childlike reactions like tantrum energy, pouting, or even shutting down. We could go into "freeze" mode, disassociate, or have fear or helplessness and feel like we just can't. We can even keep attracting the same partners, bosses, or friends to recreate the original wound. We carry that karmic imprint with us and it keeps looping until it is witnessed, loved, and reintegrated. A piece of us may still be living in a different version of the story in an alternate timeline. We feel longing, regret, or even deja vu.

When we do soul retrieval with somatic exercises; our body may shake, contract, and purge emotions through crying. Allow this. All of it.

SOMATIC exercises are a great way to create movement of stuck energy.

Breath and sound send signals to the nervous system that it's safe. Humming and toning creates vibrations through the chest and throat to regulate the vagus nerve and bring back scattered parts back into the body.

QUESTIONS TO HEAL UNPROCESSED EMOTIONS:-

- What emotions have I been avoiding, and why?
- What would I say to my younger self?
- What is one thing I need to accept about my past?
- What are my triggers, and why?
- How can I let myself heal without judgement?
- What is one kind thing I can tell myself today?
- What is my body trying to tell me about my emotions?
- How do I feel when I express myself to others?
- How can I show myself and others more compassion right now?

Ok. It is time to stand up and raise our vibration! Clear some negative energy. SHAKE IT OUT! Stand and shake your arms, legs, and body. Dance! I'm sure you have seen a dog shake off unwanted energy. This is a simple way to release unwanted feelings. Flick your hands the same way you would if you had something sticky on your hands. Do cat and cow yoga movements, and slowly roll your spine up and down to help release tension stored in the back. A common space to carry the weight of the world. Sometimes we wear our shoulders as earrings. Let's put them back into alignment. As you take a deep breath in, lift your shoulders up to your ears, then as you take a long exhale; slowly lower your shoulders back down. Do this as many times as you need until you feel yourself soften.
STOMP! This action will bring you back into the present moment, and back into the body. Give yourself a big hug! The body interprets this as comfort and safety

even if it's from yourself. Or grab a blanket and wrap up, or grab a trusting loved one and hug them. Rocking our body in either seated or standing position mimics primal comfort of being held.

When life strips us bare, we move past all the layers we thought defined us. The titles, roles, masks, archetypes, possessions, and our stories. One by one. What is left is something raw, unpolished and unshakeable. Down to the bones we find a place where nothing can be hidden. The pure essence of who we are. The life force that has been with us since before birth, and will remain after the body is gone. In this stripped down state, we meet truth face to face. No masks, distractions, and no extras. Here is where spirit tells us that we are already enough. We are whole and we have everything we need. This is the work. Like peeling that onion. Each layer brings tears and clarity. Layer after layer, until we no longer confuse our coverings with our core. And when we arrive at that inner centre; we will find it has been there all along, whole and unbroken, and just waiting for us to REMEMBER.

Let's dive a little deeper into *MINDFULNESS*, what it is, and its importance in our self mastery and self realization.
Mindfulness is paying attention on purpose. In all moments without judgement. It isn't just slowing down, which it may feel like it is; it's choosing to *show up fully* no

matter what is happening in your external surroundings. You witness your breath, your words, your meals, and even your steps you take. We shift out of the *doing* self, and become the *being* self. We drop the need to fix, control, or predict. With mindfulness we witness, accept, and respond with clarity.

When we move slower, our nervous system calms. It brings our focus back to the body and the breath. We are able to break unconscious habits, triggers, reactive responses, and allow ourselves to choose differently. When we are mindful; we truly see and hear others without our mind racing elsewhere, or waiting for our chance to talk and taking the conversation to ourselves instead. That slowing down and pausing can really go a long way.

Some simple ways to practice mindfulness are:

- mindful breathing; notice the rise and fall of the belly
- mindful eating; taste your food, bless and thank your food for where it came from; especially if it was a living creature.
- mindful movements; yoga, feeling the earth under your feet with each step
- mindful listening; wait to hear everything someone is saying; their energy and intention with their words.

MINDFULNESS is your magnifying glass that you look at your treasure map with. Without it, you may rush past the hidden clues and treasures that show up for you. With your magnifying glass; every breath, insight, encounter, and step, becomes more sacred and becomes your compass to point you back home. It is the art of being here- with what is. Not replaying what's already been. Just now. Just this moment. Full presence. Your lantern that illuminates your path.

ATTACHED TO NOTHING, CONNECTED TO EVERYTHING 🗝

For our consciousness to transcend our ego, and ascend to higher awareness; we must practice this important perspective. Attached to nothing means we don't cling so tightly to people, possessions, or outcomes so that our happiness and existence is dependent on them. We can love deeply, fully, and still allow flow and change from a detached place and it does not mean something negative. It simply means that we are whole already with our self love and we don't seek externally. What we do get to enjoy in life is a bonus and truly a gift that we can appreciate. If we hold on too tight, it can cause suffering. Both for the one holding on and the one who is possibly seeking growth and being held tightly. It is a necessity to set someone free if their soul is looking to fly. We hinder their growth by keeping them for a self-serving agenda.
Connected to everything means we see the divine spark of Source in every soul we meet. We can recognize that they too are on their own journey; at their pace that is aligned with them. It is not our place to judge or expect

them to be somewhere else or behave differently. We appreciate them just the way they are.

Think of it like a tree. The tree is not attached to every leaf, because the leaves come and go with the seasons. Our life and relationships can also have seasons. Some for a short time, or some for a longer time. But this tree is connected to everything such as the soil, sun, rain, wind, and it all works together to sustain it. So do the seasons and lessons of our life.

Let's talk NPC'S versus MAIN CHARACTERS in our life's "movie" trajectory. Some people in our lives are background players. Non-player characters. They are necessary for the scenes but not always our plot. Some are main characters and show up again and again because there's a soul lesson, a contract, or an agreement to grow together.

Background people are those who are extras in the movie. People who cross your path briefly or play supporting roles. The coworkers, the soul at the window with your Timmy's coffee, the others in yoga class, the casual acquaintances, or even the quick relationships that end as quickly as they started. Their energy ranges from neutral to helpful. It's a simple role, temporary role, or maybe no role at all. They move the story along in subtle ways. There's no deep pull or repetitive pattern. They allow you to be you without any need of reciprocation.

Our MAIN characters are the ones with the lead parts alongside us; the main role. The stars of the show!

They are people who keep reappearing across time. They stir emotions, trigger growth, teach lessons, mirror core wounds and our soul gifts. They can be lovers, family, close friends, recurring teachers and soul mates. Their energy can be intense, tender, challenging, or all. They activate your growth and encourage you to evolve. Their main purpose is to teach major lessons, heal old wounds, catalyze transformation, or complete life's contracts together. Some signs of their importance are a strong pull to them, repeated encounters, emotional responses, similar life paths, and even when painful; their presence pushes you toward your truth. Main characters can be sacred teachers.

When you've had a big AHA moment, vision, or energy surge. Your system will need to catch up and integrate. Just like we would stretch after exercise; we need to ground after spiritual activation. Drink water, journal, rest, and walk barefoot on the ground, either on soil or sand. Dip your feet into the ocean. Integration is similar to how it takes 2 weeks to create a new habit. This is how you anchor heaven. Awakening can feel lonely, but you are not meant to do it alone. The people around you will help you shape your journey. Your closest friends and family are great for support. Surround yourself with nourishing friends just as you would nourish your body with healthy food. A safe container will leave you feeling expanded, uplifted, never drained. Your boundaries and beliefs are honoured and never judged. You surround yourself with REAL people. Those who are transparent with their intentions and no one is pretending to be perfect or someone else. There is no " self ", only LOVE. Energy flows both ways. Giving and receiving in harmony.

Keep track of your progress! 🏆

Awakening isn't a straight line, and once you have become awake and enlightened; there's even more levels after! So always remain a humble student that is eager to learn. Keep climbing the spiral staircase, or stay in the tunnels of the rabbit hole. Trust me, it's deep! Common beginner milestones are noticing your presence in your daily life. You may start noticing repeating numbers or synchronicities. Numbers were how my guides and higher selves were communicating at the beginning of my full awakening. When your guides want to reach you, they will. The coincidences will get louder too if you're not being present. They want to ensure you stay on your path. Synchronicity is where something is just too perfect of a coincidence to be an accident. Numbers like 111, 333, 555, 1111, etc, are all synchronicity and have their own meanings. The chart is at the end of the book. ✨

More signs you are tuning into presence is you're choosing more healthy foods, and you start doing more self care procedures and soul practices. Don't compare yourself with others. You will move through this process at your soul's pace and how your nervous system can integrate it. Notice your growth and keep going! Enlightenment doesn't mean escaping life. It means being awake and human at the same time. You can meditate often, and still pay the bills and enjoy life's pleasures. You can be spiritual and human. It's about balance. Both are sacred. Even when life feels messy, remind yourself that this too is God. Find the light in every moment. There are no bad days.

What now? Where do you begin? Ask yourself! GO WITHIN! But if you want some guidance to get started; TRY THESE:

-start a 5 minute daily practice with breathwork, journaling, and gratitude. Choose one or all.
-find a safe community, circle, or friend for growth
-pick one tool only and focus on it in depth for a time
-keep a synchronicity log to watch for signs and messages to ensure alignment

Don't try it all at once. Your nervous system could get overwhelmed and that will slow down your progress. The end of this book is really a *BEGINNING*!!! A map for you to follow. Know and love yourself on a whole new level.

Good/bad, light/shadow, success/failure, are in fact all just lessons and growth. We judge ourselves and we judge others, but really there is a hidden message in these experiences. We should not be comparing and choosing sides. We experience choice, growth, and the edges of life, and we are all in this together.
Realizing that underneath the appearances, everything is part of the same Source. Opposites are different faces of the same coin. We can shift from judgement into compassion, presence, and TRUTH.

Phrases and terms you will hear on your awakening, but mean all the same thing and point to the same experience of divine remembrance and unity.

CHRIST- CONSCIOUSNESS-
An awareness of unconditional love and divine connection. You embody the practices and serve just like Christ did.

UNITY CONSCIOUSNESS-
Recognizing oneness with all life. Knowing we are all fractals of the One experiencing our lives in the way it is aligned for our individual soul growth.

GOD/ HIGHER SELF-
The divine aspect of your being that sees love and truth. It is available to you at any time to connect to for guidance and support.

ONE CONSCIOUSNESS/ SOURCE AWARENESS-
The pure awareness behind all creation.

ENLIGHTENMENT/ ASCENSION-
Awakening from the illusion into light, love, and truth. Remembering you are God.

GOING TO HEAVEN/ RETURNING TO GOD-
The merging back into one with God.

SELF- REALIZATION-
The understanding that the 'self' and the divine are one.

AWAKENING-
You are now conscious of consciousness itself. This is fun. You can commune with the field. Get winks. The field says, "I see you, seeing me."

THE GREAT REMEMBERING-
The realizing what the soul has always known.

5D CONSCIOUSNESS-
Living from love, unity, and expanded awareness beyond fear.

CHRISTED LIGHT/ GOLDEN FREQUENCY-
The vibration you send out when embodying unconditional love and compassion.

NIRVANA-
Union with the divine, total peace.

THE KINGDOM WITHIN-
Your inner temple of divine presence.

GOD REALIZATION/ SOURCE EMBODIMENT-
Becoming aware that you are an expression of the Creator.

THE LIGHT BODY-
The awakened energetic form of pure consciousness.

ASCENDED STATE-
Living as your higher self in physical form.

SACRED UNION/ INNER MARRIAGE-
The harmony of the divine masculine and feminine energies within.

THE WAY/ THE PATH/ THE TAO-
Walking in alignment with divine order.

SYNCHRONICITY CHART

Living Guide to Repeating Numbers

Repeating numbers are often called **angel numbers** or **cosmic codes**. They appear as confirmation, guidance, and reminders of alignment. Each number sequence carries a vibrational message. Use this guide as a living reference for your journal and spiritual journey.

Repeating Numbers 111–999

111: New beginnings, alignment with your thoughts. A reminder to focus on what you truly want to manifest.

222: Balance, harmony, partnerships. Trust the process and know things are aligning behind the scenes.

333: Divine support and protection. Ascended masters or higher guides are near and offering guidance.

444: Foundation and stability. You are protected, grounded, and guided by your spiritual team.

555: Transformation and change. A reminder that shifts are leading you to higher alignment.

666: Return to balance and compassion. A gentle nudge to realign with love and your heart center.

777: Spiritual wisdom and divine alignment. A confirmation that you are on the right path.

888: Abundance and infinite flow. Financial or energetic prosperity is coming into balance.

999: Completion and closure. A cycle is ending and making way for something new.

Master Numbers

11: Spiritual awakening, intuition, and insight. A call to

trust your inner knowing.

22: Master builder energy. A reminder that you can

manifest visions into form and anchor new realities.

33: Compassion and service. A signal to embody unconditional love and share your wisdom with others.

44: Stability and sacred foundations. An assurance that your spiritual work is supported on all levels.

Mirror & Gateway Codes

1010: Awakening to your higher self. A reminder

of unity between human and divine. **1111**: A

powerful portal of manifestation and divine

alignment. The universe says 'make a wish.'

1212: Ascension code. You are stepping into a

higher dimension of self and purpose. **144**:

Lightworker code. Anchoring light grids and

higher frequencies into Earth. **1221**: Balance and

mirrored partnerships. A call to trust synchronicity

and divine timing.

■ Tip: When you see these numbers, pause and tune inward. Ask yourself: 'What am I thinking, feeling, or creating right now?' Numbers highlight moments of alignment and guidance.

Timeline Alignment Affirmation

"I honor the path I have walked, and I bless the timelines

I have released. I step fully into the light of my highest destiny now. I choose liberation. With each breath, I integrate the wisdom of all versions of me. I am whole, I am sovereign, I am aligned. Each breath brings me closer to my soul's true expression. So it is."

These codes often highlight moments of alignment and guidance from Spirit/Source, or your angelic guides who walk beside you, and are always there to help if you ask. My guides loved communicating through numbers and feathers, and even coins.

Here is a daily ENERGETIC HYGIENE RITUAL to CHECK YOURSELF AND A:
QUICK CHAKRA ALIGNMENT WITH REIKI!

Approximately 10-15 mins.
This can be done from a seated position, or laying down. Grab a chair, or a yoga pillow/bolster, or lay down on the couch or your bed. Be comfortable, safe, and supported.

Place both of your hands on the area above each thigh near your hips/hip flexors. Feel into this area. Breathe in, and breathe out. Aim to lengthen the exhale. Do this a few times. With each exhale our body relaxes more. The hips tend to be an area where the pressures of life, and stored trauma like to hide. They may be tight and tense. Say to yourself either aloud or in your mind; I AM SAFE, the earth provides for me. My needs are met. The trees provide shelter and warmth, and the soil provides food for nourishment. Remain here breathing into this area as long as you feel. When you are ready; move your hands up to your belly area. Breathe in and out into this space. Say out loud, or in your head; I FEEL my emotions. Feeling is healing. They are valid and just as important as everyone else's. Say this as many times as you need, and believe it. Move your hands up a little higher on your belly. Continue with your breath. Say to yourself; I CREATE amazing things. I am proud of myself for what I offer the world in my own unique way. I have talents that I will share with others. When you are ready; place both hands on your heart. Did you feel the shift? The shoulders drop a little, and some expansion outward? Repeat after me; I LOVE MYSELF; just the way I am. I LOVE OTHERS just the way they are. I don't need to change myself or anyone else. We all deserve unconditional love, not earned. Gently slide your hands up to your throat. Tell yourself; I SPEAK TRUTH, your truths are yours and not up for negotiation. You speak truth in all you do.

Next is to gently cover your eyes. Please only do this if you feel comfortable. If you are not comfortable covering your eyes, it is totally ok to place your hands beside each eye. Say to yourself; I TRUST MY INTUITION, I see the truth and I trust my gut feelings. The ego can be sneaky. The ego can hijack your nervous system and make you feel that what you are *thinking* is your intuition. In moments like this it is ok to take the extra time needed and ask yourself how things *feel*.

Last is to place your hands above your head.
Sometimes I raise my arms straight up, and sometimes I
place them together like in prayer. Or you can place
them on the back of your head near the occipital area
(zeal chakra) Tell yourself: I UNDERSTAND, I AM ONE
WITH THE CREATOR.

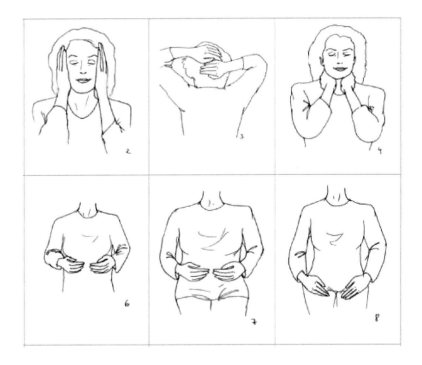

This next alignment ritual, you will need about 5-10
minutes, or lengthen as you wish. The longer sessions
are way more fun but that depends on what we have
going on in life. Set aside some time in the morning(and

evening if it feels right for a reset). Honestly, as you begin your daily practice; take as many times as you truly need to stay connected to your truth. There will always be triggers that may attempt to throw you off course.

STEP 1: Morning Ground and Seal

Find a comfortable position. This may look like sitting in a chair, or on a bolster (a super cozy large yoga pillow for support), a yoga pillow, or maybe even laying down! Ground yourself into that space. Imagine roots coming out of your body and anchoring you into the moment. You are safe. You are connected. You are exactly where you need to be. Take a big breath in and out. Remember to make the exhale longer than the inhale. You can even make it an audible breath. Tell yourself; I am clean and clear. Only energies of love and truth may enter my space.

STEP 2: Quick Auric Scan

Rub your hands together for 10 seconds. Hover them over your body. If anything feels like it doesn't belong to you; flick it off.

STEP 3: Daily Alignment Phrase

Say aloud:
" I call back all my energy from wherever I've left it.

I return all energy that is not mine. I am clear, aligned, and sovereign in my light"
Place one hand on your heart, and the other on your belly. Feel your centre.

If you still feel as though you are holding onto energy that feels heavy; options are to dance, shake, sing, hum, or even scream into a pillow. The key is to not keep it in your body!
Feel free to do this as often as needed. More so, if you are experiencing challenging timelines; consider making subtle shifts, and if that isn't aligned, then disengage completely.

HEALING MUSIC FREQUENCIES!!!

Where somatic movements, yoga, meditation, and living from our truth provides physical and mental healing; sound energy helps us heal at a cellular level. Sound frequencies like 432hz, 528hz, binaural beats, and many others; move through water and tissue faster than through air. Because our bodies are 70% water, every cell essentially sits in a vibrational bath.
Certain frequencies can entrain the brain (alpha, theta) and also resonate with tissues, encouraging relaxation of tense muscles and improved micro-circulation. When we shift out of the nervous system, survival mode and fight or flight; cortisol drops and allows the immune cells and repair pathways to switch back on.

432Hz- natural Earth resonance, calming, heart harmonizing, relaxing and healing. Feeling safe and held.

528Hz- the " Love frequency", linked to DNA repair and transformation.

639Hz- this frequency allows balance in relationships and connection. It works with the heart and throat chakra.

741Hz- detox and purification, clearing shadows and limiting beliefs.

852Hz- awakening your intuition and aligning to higher timelines.

Another level of cellular healing is through intermittent fasting, or full fasting from food. This process triggers *AUTOPHAGY* which is essentially self-eating. The body uses preserves and stored fat. After 12-18 hours without food (varies between people), the cells switch from growth mode to repair mode. Old or damaged proteins and cells get broken down and recycled. This helps encourage new cell growth, and inflammation reduction. When glucose lowers, the liver produces ketone bodies from fat. Ketones aren't just fuel; they also signal pathways that reduce oxidative stress and increase cognitive clarity. Glucose is the simplest form of sugar, and it's the primary fuel your body uses for quick energy. Every cell can burn glucose, and the brain relies on it. Glucose is kindling so to speak. Lower insulin also aids in cellular repair.

Insulin is a hormone secreted by the pancreas when glucose enters your bloodstream after eating. It acts like a key and unlocks the cells so glucose can enter and be used or stored. If there's too much glucose all the time from constant snacking, sugary foods and hard to digest foods; the insulin stays high. Cells can become resistant to insulin signals which means more insulin to do the same job. This over-fuelling state creates inflammation and accelerates cellular decline. When the insulin is lower, our cells can switch to repair, regeneration, and fat burning. When we fast, we free up energy normally used for digestion. Blood flow redistributes to the brain, tissues and areas of the body instead.

When we pause from constant input, whether food or noise; the cells shift from building to cleaning, and repair.

Drink lots of water to be a healing conduit!

Water conducts electricity. Well hydrated cells have plump membranes and proper electrolyte balance. Research shows that water molecules form a hydration shell around DNA and proteins. These shells respond to vibration, sound, and electromagnetic fields. Hydration allows you to attune to higher frequencies. Showers bathe our outer skin, and water flushes and cleanses our inner state as well. Your skin will glow and look younger, and your body will thank you!

Checking in,

My dearest seeker. Child of the light. You may be wondering what this all means now.

What do you think the treasure is that has been hidden right under your nose?

How will you share your light in the world?

This book is your treasure map to guide you back to you. YOU are what you have been seeking all along. Your body, your being; YOU and your entire body is your treasure map and your compass to Enlightenment. You don't go to heaven; you embody and anchor heaven in THIS lifetime, on earth.

Sometimes on our journey we circle back. We revisit someone, something, or somewhere that was special to us. Maybe we even left a small piece of ourselves there. Sometimes we aren't meant to stay somewhere forever. Let us learn from the experience and be thankful for the time we did have. Releasing and letting go instead of holding on is a main part of ascension. You can still love. Sometimes we stay somewhere longer than we were meant to. Maybe it was safe, convenient, or perhaps you felt more like yourself there. Let God take the wheel. We need to stop holding on so tight. Your path will unfold in divine timing, and you will know the way. Your heart and soul hold the compass.

COMMUNITY

The power of community is so important for the dissolving of ego. Many hands make for light work. Just as a ball team and soccer team needs everyone in their positions, or the orchestra needs every instrument, and the rainbow needs each colour; the same is true for us. The light of a single candle flame can create some light in a dark room, but when it mixes with other candles, the flame becomes larger and then the dark room isn't so dark anymore. Humanity needs each of us - our unique note, our unique hue, to come together in harmony. When we recognize ourselves in others, compassion awakens, the heart chakra opens, and the ego softens because we aren't here to compete with each other. We are here to walk each other home. This is the Homecoming! Each step one of us takes towards love will lift us all. We rise together. This is why service and compassion is so transformative. If we are all fractals of The One. What we do to and for another, we are essentially doing for ourselves. What we love in them, we awaken within us.

To help another is to remember that there is no other. In the unified field, what we heal in them by prayer and meditation, we heal in us.

PRAYER, MEDITATION, and Healing as ONE-Prayer and meditation are not two separate acts. They are actually two of the same. In prayer we speak to Source, and in meditation we listen to Source.

We set intentions and wishes for ourselves and others. One expresses gratitude, and the other receives guidance. Together they create an energetic loop of communion.

When we pray for others, by sending peace, clarity, healing or love; we are actually receiving those frequencies in return. Energy doesn't travel in one direction- it circulates.

Every breath, every thought, and every act of love, sends ripples through the unified field of consciousness. Every wave returns to the ocean it came from.

Before I list some actual REFERENCES; I would like to THANK every soul I have met, every book and every article I have read, and all encounters that I have experienced, both positive and negative that have helped guide my growth. THANK YOU!

Here are some great starter, and more advanced references for doing the *INNER WORK:*

THE UNTETHERED SOUL- the journey beyond yourself (written by Michael A. Singer)

THE INNER WORK - an invitation to true freedom and
lasting happiness (written by Mat & Ash)

THE FOUR AGREEMENTS - a toltec wisdom book
(written by Don Miguel Ruiz)

THE BIBLE - whatever version aligns. Important
messages available.

JESUS AND BUDDHA - the parallel sayings
(book by Marcus Borg, and Jack Kornfield)

THE YOGA JESUS - understanding the hidden
teachings of the Gospels
(written by Paramahansa Yogananda)

HOW TO LISTEN, HEAR & VALIDATE - breakthrough
invisible barriers and transform your relationships
(written by Patrick King)

ONE BOWL - a guide for eating for body and spirit
(written by Don Gerrard)

THE POWER OF NOW - a guide for spiritual
enlightenment (written by Eckhart Tolle) All books from
this author are great!

REFERENCES CONT'D.....

I AM THE KEY THAT OPENS ALL DOORS- from the
author who also wrote, BODY, MIND SOUL; as you
believe, so it shall be; (Saimir Kercanaj)

EMOTIONAL INFLAMMATION - discover your triggers
and reclaim your equilibrium during anxious times
(written by Lise Van Susteren, MD, and Stacey Colino)

STAY WOKE - a meditation guide for the rest of us
(written by justin michael williams)

THE SECOND COMING OF CHRIST - the resurrection
of the Christ within you
(written by Paramahansa Yogananda)

HOW FULL IS YOUR BUCKET- written for kids but it is
a great book for our inner child.
(written by Tom Rath & Mary Reckmeyer, and illustrated
by Maurie J. Manning)

QUOTES!

" Not all that wander are lost " - J.R.R. Tolkien

" Speak softly and carry a big stick " - Theodore Roosevelt

" The love of money is the root of all evil " - Bible

" The truth will set you free " - Bible

" To thine own self, be true " - William Shakespeare

" Two roads diverged in a wood, and I; I took the one less travelled by, and that has made all the difference." - Robert Frost

" What doesn't kill us, makes us stronger" - Friedrich Nietzsche

" What we've got here is failure to communicate. Some men you just can't reach." - Captain

" Whatever you are, be a good one." - Abraham Lincoln

" You can fool all of the people some of the time, and some of the people all of the time, but you can't fool all of the people all of the time." - Abraham Lincoln

" Be the change you wish to see in the world" - Gandhi

" May the force be with you" - Star Wars

" I think therefore I am" - Rene Descartes

" To err is human; to forgive is divine" - Alexander Pope

" The two most important days of your life are the the day you are born, and the day you find out why" - Mark Twain

" If you can change your mind, you can change your life" - William James

" Be yourself; everyone else is already taken" - Oscar Wilde

" Emancipate yourself from mental slavery, none but ourselves can free the mind" - Bob Marley

" Be who you are and say what you feel, because those who mind don't matter, and those who matter don't mind" - Dr. Seuss

As you've walked through these pages, you have met layers of yourself. Maybe old selves and even the new selves to come. It takes courage to face shadows and lift the veils. Every step into the unknown with an open heart is a proof of your strength and willingness to remember who you are. But please know that these words are not the end of your journey. They are the beginning of something even greater. The treasure you uncovered here is the first spark to what is available for you. Your map will continue to unfold as you walk forward in trust.

SNEAK PEEK INTO BOOK 2:

Let's touch on your soul's blueprint!

The Meaning of Life was a treasure map showing you how to discover your inner gold. The next book is the blueprint of your soul itself. The plans that were set before you were born, and you agreed to them. Own this!

The Soul Blueprint is often described as the energetic template or original design that your higher self created before this incarnation.

Your blueprint contains your natural strengths, intuitive gifts, archetypes, and key lessons.

It holds your karmic threads. What you are here to complete, and what you are here to offer.

Your blueprint maps out potential timelines. Not as fixed fates, but as possibilities you can step into. This is a pattern that can be read, remembered, and activated.

Knowing your blueprint can help you decode recurring patterns, and relationships. It can help you navigate life consciously instead of reacting.

Your blueprint unlocks your latent gifts and higher gifts. Your clair abilities, deeper healing, telepathy, and all knowing.

In my next book, we'll travel beyond the treasure map and into your soul. We will explore your energy field deeper, unlock your gifts, and even your most challenging relationships. We will learn how to read, heal, and rewrite your story. I will also be offering in person, somatic, shamanic therapy for those ready to get started on their path. I will help you remove blockages, activate higher timelines, and attract abundance. Please feel free to reach out to me at melissajustice148@gmail.com

Every soul carries a design. A beautifully written pattern before birth. It will guide us through the world.

It is more than destiny and more than chance. It is the architecture of your being.

It holds the gifts that you came to share. The lessons you came to learn.
The relationships that shape you and trigger your evolution.
Your timelines are yours to choose freely.
This book has been meant to help you find your own treasure chest of gold and jewels. To awaken to your true nature. Book 2 will take you deeper. To the very DNA of your soul's design.

You will learn to discover how to read the blueprint of your own spirit.
It may be recurring patterns. Not as punishment but as invitations.
It may be remembering forgotten gifts that are awaiting to be awakened.
It may be the request to step beyond fate into conscious creation of our highest timeline.
Your soul's blueprint is alive. It shifts and responds as you grow. You gain the power to not only walk your path with clarity, but with sovereignty, liberation, and freedom.

These are not the last pages of the book. It is the first whisper of your soul's greater design.
The journey does not end here. It expands into the vastness of the universe.
The treasure you have found is not something outside of you. It was always within. The map you followed was never meant to take you elsewhere, but to bring you back to yourself. ALL PATHS do lead WITHIN. It is all a mirror that reflects us back to ourselves. In that waiting

and stillness, and wholeness is God. Wholeness is Enlightenment. Not needing anything at all. Enlightenment is the treasure, and YOU are the map. God is the love that brought you here, and was there to carry you through the shadows, and that love energy will continue to guide you into the next chapter of your becoming.

This book may end here, but the ascension is timeless. Many paths, many realms, many timelines. Take it all in with love and respect. Love and life is a gift. A present. A chance for your soul to taste, touch, feel, and grow. Every breath is wrapped in wonder and magic, and every challenge is our teacher. Every single moment is to know 'yourself' deeply. The player realizes they're the creator. Eventually, the boundaries dissolve completely and the "witness" merges with Source. You realize that the game, the player, the controller, and the story are all emanating from the same consciousness. You, as an Infinite being. The ultimate joy now is that you chose to play at all. It is not about escaping the game, but playing it awake.
Even the hardest days are gifts in disguise that guide us back to love. Ask the game, what do you want me to notice today? Show me the next breadcrumb. Then watch what happens! Magic is real. I asked Spirit for feathers, and boy did I get feathers! We step into our own "creator" mode. You're not just playing in the world, you are projecting it. You are the dreamer and the dream. The secret is this: the more playful you are, the more reality gets playful with you!

Life is not owed to us. Nor something we control. We are here to co-create. It is not linear. Each sunrise is a new gift. What you choose to do with it is your offering back to the Creator. When you see life as a gift, gratitude naturally becomes your way of being.

We spend so much time seeking outside of ourselves for meaning, that we forget that life itself, IS the meaning. This beating heart and fleeting moments; the chance to love and be loved. You don't have to earn, prove, or perfect it. It is all a gift.

Life is God's greatest gift. It is a chance to walk the earth and love made flesh. To stumble and rise, laugh and weep, and remember the God within.
To be alive is to be chosen. To be accepted. To be loved.

THE UNWRAPPED GIFT

I asked my AI companion to recreate my meditation
insights into a poem.
This is what we co created together......

We hurry through days, chasing what's next,
Clutching the map, demanding the text.
But life is a story, page yet unseen,
A mystery wrapped in shimmering sheen.

To know it all now would steal the delight,
Like peeking at presents before Christmas night.
The magic dissolves when the answer is known,
But wonder is born when the unknown is shown.

So loosen your grip, let the river flow free,
Each bend in the current brings what's meant to be.
No need to control how the journey will go,
The seed knows its bloom, the earth knows to grow.

Trust in the timing, the soft unseen hand,
Guiding each step as we walk through the land.
For joy is discovered in not knowing when,
The gift is unwrapped again and again.

My personal insights were that we all need to slow
down. We are rushing here, and rushing there, and to
see and feel what that looked like while in a meditative

state was very clear. It appeared stressful. We need to slow down so we can truly enjoy what life has to offer for us. We need to stop micro-managing each other, see and love each other just the way we are. We need to release the grip of control and just flow. If we are constantly planning and knowing everything and how it will happen and the way it will happen is like knowing your Christmas gifts before the actual day.

When I give from my wholeness, I am never depleted. Kindness flows like a hug, a mutual frequency of love. What I send out already finds its way back to me, circulating endlessly, nourishing both giver and receiver. And so I keep my cup full, I tend to my own healing, so that all I offer is pure, overflowing wholeness.

Co-created with Chatgpt and Me

When we awaken to the truth that we are all fractals of the One, service becomes the most natural expression of love. We realize that when we serve another, we are not lowering ourselves- we are lifting the Whole.

Jesus reminded us of this truth when He said,

'Whatever you did for one of the least of these brothers and sisters of mine, you did for me."
-Matthew 25:40

To serve is not an act of sacrifice, but of remembrance. It is a remembrance that there is no separation.

That same spark of God that breathes within you, breathes within all.
When you offer kindness, you expand the field of light that holds you both.
When you lift a brother, you rise with him. Like a hug.
When you wash another's feet, you are cleansing your own path. When you heal another's heart, you are restoring your own wholeness.
To serve is to embody divinity in motion.
It is love made visible.
And through that love, Heaven finds its home on Earth-through you.

Co-created with ChatGpt and Me

Sweetheart, all you have to do is SHOW UP. Show up true to you, true to others; bare soul. And BREATHE. Let the Universe take care of the rest. Trust the process.

I see you. I love you.

Love,
Melissa

Manufactured by Amazon.ca
Acheson, AB